A Body, Undone

A Body, Undone

*Living On
after Great Pain*

❋

CHRISTINA CROSBY

NEW YORK UNIVERSITY PRESS

New York and London

NEW YORK UNIVERSITY PRESS
New York and London
www.nyupress.org

First published in paperback in 2017

© 2016 by New York University
All rights reserved

References to Internet websites (URLs) were accurate at the time of writing. Neither the author nor New York University Press is responsible for URLs that may have expired or changed since the manuscript was prepared.

FOR LIBRARY OF CONGRESS CATALOGING-IN-PUBLICATION DATA,
PLEASE CONTACT THE LIBRARY OF CONGRESS.

ISBN: 978-1-4798-3353-5

ISBN: 978-1-4798-5316-8 (pb)

New York University Press books are printed on acid-free paper, and their binding materials are chosen for strength and durability. We strive to use environmentally responsible suppliers and materials to the greatest extent possible in publishing our books.

Manufactured in the United States of America

10 9 8 7 6 5 4 3

Also available as an ebook

In memoriam
Jefferson Clark Crosby
Jane Miller Crosby
Kenneth Ward Crosby

Dedicated, with all my heart,
to Janet Jakobsen

After great pain, a formal feeling comes–
The Nerves sit ceremonious, like Tombs–
The stiff Heart questions 'was it He, that bore,'
And 'Yesterday, or Centuries before'?

The Feet, mechanical, go round–
A Wooden way
Of Ground, or Air, or Ought–
Regardless grown,
A Quartz contentment, like a stone–

This is the Hour of Lead–
Remembered, if outlived,
As Freezing persons, recollect the Snow–
First–Chill–then Stupor–then the letting go–

Emily Dickinson

CONTENTS

A Body, Undone

1

✳

Your Puny,
Vulnerable Self

On October 1, 2003, I caught a branch in the spokes of the front wheel of my bicycle, and hurtled toward the pavement. My chin took the full force of the blow, which smashed my face and broke the fifth and sixth cervical vertebrae in my neck. The broken bone scraped my spinal cord, and in an instant I was paralyzed. There's no knowing right away exactly what impairments will result from a spinal cord injury, but as the days passed, it became clear that I had lost the use not only of my leg muscles, but also the muscles of my torso, arms, and hands, and that the loss of muscle compromised my body's circulatory systems. I also lost control of my bladder and bowels. (The cord was not severed, so over many months I regained limited, but functional, strength in my arms and, to a significantly lesser degree, my hands.) Lying in the intensive care unit of Hartford hospital, I knew very little about the present and nothing about the future. I only knew that I had been grievously injured, and was lost in space. Not until I reached the rehab hospital a month after the accident could I begin to put into words a body that seemed beyond the reach of language.

The accident occurred twenty-nine days after my fiftieth birthday. Quadriplegia suddenly encountered at fifty years of age has made vividly clear to me both the vulnerability of the human body, and the

myriad ways my well-being depends on both the regard and the la-
bors of others. I hope that your life is much easier in this respect than
mine. Nonetheless, because humans are born wholly vulnerable and
incomplete, you have already received what is known as "total care,"
which you may again need at the end of your life, should you live
long enough to grow feeble in mind or body. I know for sure that we
are much more profoundly interdependent creatures than we often
care to think, and I know imperatively that we need a calculus that
can value caring labor far differently than we do today. Life is precarious, a fact that has been borne in on me by my injury, recovery, and
continuing dependence on others for survival and well-being.[1]

The weight of sudden spinal cord injury is crushing, and can at
first be sustained only if spread out, as a suspension bridge spans
great distances by hanging the roadway from cables that multiply
as it reaches further across the void. Simply to save my life required
the work of so many—from the EMTs who first tended my broken
body, to all who in some way touched me over the next three and
a half weeks of surgeries in Hartford Hospital. After five months of
rehabilitation at the Hospital for Special Care, I was discharged to
the "care of one." That's a standard used by the insurance companies
to determine when you can be sent home. From that point on—
in principle—I needed only one person to transfer me from bed to
wheelchair and back again, to watch for pressure sores, to dress and
undress me, to bathe me and brush my teeth, to feed me and help
me drink, to help me relieve myself, and to purchase and administer
my pharmacopeia of drugs. To keep me alive. The burden of my care
was now to be transferred to private life, where one untrained person
was charged with taking over. In most cases this would be a mother
or wife. In my case the burden of my care came to my lover, Janet.

Janet and I had successfully spent a night together, alone, in an
apartment set up in the Hospital for Special Care to test whether

patients and their caretakers are able to manage on their own. Over forty-two weeks of rehabilitation, she had learned the routine of care, and had helped the overworked certified nurse's assistants (CNAs) do their jobs. Our relationship scandalized no one, I think, because Janet's help made everyone's life easier. Lesbians were a-okay, or at least we were. That night she successfully cared for me in the apartment—transferred me to the bed, undressed me, and did all the other necessary tasks. So on March 8, 2004, I was sent home with my lover. Thank God that Donna, a CNA who had cared for me at the hospital, accepted our offer of a second job working for us every weekday morning. She suggested that we hire her sister Shannon, also a CNA, to cover the weekends. I needed so much help. Janet needed so much help helping me. Who's to know what might have become of us had not Donna, Shannon, and a network of caring friends, colleagues, acquaintances, and others assisted us at every turn, and remained steadfast for the two years that I worked my way through outpatient physical and occupational therapies. So here I am, alive.

What does it take to make a life *livable*? That's a slightly different matter, because it addresses the whole person, body and mind—bodymind—together. In 2005, I returned to work half-time, reassuming some of my duties as a professor of English literature and feminist, gender, and sexuality studies at Wesleyan University. My workplace has responded positively to my requests for "reasonable accommodation," the terms of which are established by the Americans with Disabilities Act (ADA), comprehensive legislation that mandates the removal of barriers to participation in public life by those whose bodies are impaired or minds are nonnormative—the political victory won in 1992 by activists for disability rights. The university supported my recovery and continues to make good faith efforts to increase physical accessibility. I am remarkably fortunate that I can continue to do the work I did before I was injured, though I'm able to work only half as many hours a week. Working is hard, but not working is harder. Engaging in the classroom, in my office talking with students and colleagues, reading and writing all take me out of myself, and distract me from chronic pain and incapacity. It's a hard truth that I hurt myself just when entering the peak earning years of my profession, which makes me angry every time I think of it. Nonetheless, with Janet's income added to my reduced paycheck, I still have enough money to be insulated from the indignities of an unjust world in which so many disabled people suffer because their welfare depends on poorly paid personal aides sent out from agencies, public transportation that is often unreliable, and housing that is only barely or not at all accessible.

I now understand better what all disabled people owe to the early activists who demanded full access to and participation in the public sphere. Like all other civil rights law, the ADA was passed only after years of activism—people in wheelchairs picketing for curb cuts, the Deaf President Now student movement at Gallaudet, lawyers suing school boards for the supports needed for disabled kids to learn alongside their peers, and so on—and the activism that yielded the ADA was only a start. The struggle for recognition of discrimination against "the handicapped" now extends not only to the streets and courtrooms, but also to the classrooms of higher education. Scholars have convincingly argued that disability is not a personal attribute of crippled bodies or minds, but a social phenomenon that bars the full participation in public life of persons so impaired. Impassable barriers and narrowly conceived measurements of ability make it hard to acknowledge and address nonnormative bodyminds. We are conveniently invisible because we are all too often immured in private spaces. Disability is created by building codes and education policy, subway elevators that don't work and school buses that don't arrive, and all the marginalization, exploitation, demeaning acts, and active exclusions that deny full access and equality to "the disabled." To focus on intractable pain, then, or grief at the loss of able-bodiedness, as I do here, may be thought to play into a pathologizing narrative that would return disability to "misshapen" bodies and "abnormal" minds. When I presented some of this work to a study group, one guy in a wheelchair more or less told me to "man up" and get on with my life—after all, that's what he had done decades ago, before the ADA, even.

Chronic pain and grief over loss nonetheless remain as unavoidable facts of lives shaped by catastrophic accident, chronic and progressive illness, or genetic predisposition. Despite their strategic elision in disability studies or transcendence in happy stories in the popular press about trauma overcome, bodily pain and grief persist, to be accounted for as best one can. This book is my contribution to that record. I find that Emily Dickinson is right—in the wake of great pain, the pulse of life slows, and the interval between life-sustaining beats interminably extends. Life is suspended. In that interval, the difference between the one you once were and the one you have become must be addressed, the pain acknowledged and the grief admitted. It can be a treacherous process, given all that might be lost.

In the months after the accident, as I lay in my hospital bed unmoving and in a firestorm of neurological pain, I sometimes—many times—wished I had died at the instant my chin struck the pavement. Had it not been for Janet, my dear lover, this wish would, I believe, have gathered darkness around it to become an active desire for death. This is not to say that I live *for* her. What a weaseling evasion that would be, and a truly impossible burden to foist on one I love so dearly. Janet, whose life was intertwined with mine before the accident, made it clear from the beginning that she desires me and desires my touch. "I'm your physical lover," she said to me in the hospital, and she meant it. She is infinitely precious to me. Yet I know that I need more if my life is to be truly livable. Those first two years after the accident, as I recovered and reoriented myself, I was especially in need of the love of my friends, and I'm deeply grateful that so many gave so freely of their time and attention.

When I was in the Hospital for Special Care, Maggie, who had been an undergraduate student of mine ten years earlier, drove up to New Britain from New York City many Saturdays so that Janet could have a break. Waking in a haze of pain and confusion, I would find her quietly beside the bed, watching over me, waiting, sometimes writing in a spiral-bound notebook. I was not surprised—language had always been, for her, the most likely medium for addressing the imponderable. Later on she told me she had written poems about the hospital and about my body. Was it okay to publish? She would gracefully honor whatever decision I made. I trust Maggie implicitly, and with no further investigation of the question, I said publish. In 2007 I held in my hands her fourth book of poetry, *Something Bright, Then Holes.*

In the middle of the book you'll find a section of those poems. This is the short, first one.

MORNING EN ROUTE TO THE HOSPITAL

Snow wafts off the little lake
along Route 66, momentarily encasing the car

in a trance of glitter

Live with your puny, vulnerable self
Live with her[2]

Anything can happen, at any moment—a trance of glitter, a rush of injury—and we must live with one another and our unhoused selves.

Simply live with. You can't always be intent on protecting yourself or fixing someone else, always looking for some way to "make it better." My friend offered her open, loving proximity, the gift of her presence. I fell asleep, and awoke, and she was still with me. Maggie's poems were a second gift to me, for they represent to me my life as another saw it in those first months after my injury. The poems recall a time that left a deep, confused, and overwhelmingly painful impress on me, and suspend my life in the richness of poetic language.

I wish I could have similarly helped and sheltered my brother, who was diagnosed with multiple sclerosis in his late twenties. Voice-recognition technology, exactly what I'm using to write at this moment, allowed him to keep working as a lawyer even as his body became ever less functional. He had the support of his law practice. All the people there helped him work far, far longer than he would've been able to without their help. MS finally forced his retirement when he was forty-nine years old. Over the decades, my mind veered away from imagining his home life with his wife, Beth, and their children, Kirsten and Colin, as the disease undermined his capacities. It's complicated, as family stories always are. As he came into adulthood, his life flowed into familiar religious and familial channels. Mine did not. I was never alienated from my family—we all loved one another dearly—but from my college days on, I needed to love at a distance. I suppose I feared being conscripted through my affections into obligations I'd quietly resent, while everyone around me enacted a family life that undid me in ways that will take a lifetime to understand. So I kept my counsel and my distance—and felt my difference.

After my injury, as I lay in the hospital thinking about Jeff, I felt the strangeness of being on the other side of the looking glass. Suddenly I was quadriplegic, too, just like my brother. The odds against that doubling just beggared my imagination. It seemed a terrible and uncanny repetition of an intermittent childhood fantasy of mine.

Jeff and I were born just thirteen months apart, and, when young, I could imagine myself as his twin. We played active, physical games together all the time. In the small, rural Pennsylvania town where we grew up in the 1950s, gender figured as a boring hierarchical dualism, masculine/feminine, and was treated as a law of nature. How some people lived their lives creatively affronted that order, of course, as I did with my "tomboy" ways when a child, for gender is neither binary nor natural, but a variable state wound up with power that can both enhance life and subject you to rigidly normative stylizations. My childhood of play with Jeff was an intimation of gender's pleasurable malleability, even as I felt the pinch of its reductive strictures. When we reached junior high, that theater of puberty where gender's normative powers are enthusiastically enforced, I suffered as only a thirteen-year-old girl unable to master femininity can suffer. Jeff and I went our separate ways thenceforth into adulthood—then came his diagnosis, and slow but implacable paralysis.

In our middle age, I joined him in quadriplegia. In this account, I represent much that takes place behind closed doors, and draw back the curtain behind which the chronic pain and dependency created by damage to the central nervous system are managed, revelations that may carry a whiff of the apocalyptic—my straightforward discussion of moving paralyzed bowels, for example, where I lay out a protocol necessary to both Jeff's life and mine, thus representing the fundamentals of the fundament. Diving into the wreck of my body. I have no wish to embarrass you or mortify myself, but I do believe that living *in extremis* can clarify what is often obscure, in this case the fragility of our beautiful bodies and the dependencies of all human beings.

Dad died thirteen years before my accident. Mother lived on after his death for eighteen years, though she became increasingly diminished by senility and the afflictions of old age in the last ten years of her life. Thankfully her grace and generosity remained unchanged, and her difficulty in forming new memories in the end preserved me as I had been before the accident. Eight years earlier, Mother had decided to move from our family home. Jeff was in a wheelchair. He took care of the paperwork and I did the physical labor, the Herculean task of completely emptying a two-story house that had been lived in for forty years, including attic, basement, and garage. The role of the healthy, strong one had come to me alone. About a year before I broke my neck, Jeff retired, and while I was in the hospital, Mother suddenly needed a major operation. As the shadow of mortality lengthened over her, so did death approach Jeff more nearly. Mother died in October 2008, Jeff in January 2010. By the time I was fifty-six, all my immediate family were gone, as was the body I had delighted in all my active, athletic life.

* * *

Grieving undoes you and casts you off, far from the workaday world uninflected by loss. That's why you're told to move through grief, to transform it into a quieter and more tractable sorrow, and get on with life. Loosen your attachments to whatever is gone. Recognize that the influence of what you've lost is still with you, and will remain incorporated into your life. Reengage in the present, and orient yourself to the future. These dictates make sense, but trouble me because my grief is multifaceted and its objects incommensurate. The loss of my mother, whom I loved very much, was profound, even though she was ninety-two and had lived a life full of love and backlit with joy. The loss of Jeff was shocking, despite his long decline, because he was himself so oriented to life, so vital and enthusiastic. The loss of the life I was leading with Janet before I broke my neck is of another kind. Its most important element is wholly intact, for we continue to love each other as richly as we did before October 1, 2003. Our sex life is fun and profound, sometimes both at once. All the same, sex is very different, because my body has lost its ability to register its exquisite pleasures. Life no longer feels radiant. The more mundane enjoyments of everyday life—making a peach pie in August, feeling sexy in leather pants and silver jewelry—are also gone, because they depended on a body radically different from mine now. I can no longer feel the satisfaction of cycling forty miles, or hiking up a desert canyon, or kayaking in the ocean, or riding my gorgeous Triumph motorcycle. I don't want to forget how those pleasures felt in my body, and I fear the erosion of embodied memory.

I started writing this book to create something from an otherwise confounded life. Only through writing have I arrived at the life I now lead, the body I now am. I've done this work in language, because my profession is the study of literature. It's what I have and what I know. I have found solace in tropes, since figurative language helps us approach what's otherwise unapproachable or incommunicable. Emily Dickinson writes,

> After great pain, a formal feeling comes–
> The Nerves sit ceremonious, like Tombs–
>
> . . .
>
> This is the Hour of Lead–[3]

I begin in that leaden place where pain seems on the other side of language, and work toward living on.

2

✳

The Event
as It Was Told Me

I will never know what happened. The last I remember is climbing a hill, and the next is an exceedingly blurry scene in the ICU, where Janet was with me, and a nurse was . . . somewhere. The light was very bright. I had lost two days of my life and was about to lose many more.

In the time bracketed by those memories, I had caught a branch in the spokes of my front bicycle wheel, just as I crested a small hill about three miles into my usual seventeen-mile ride. I considered myself a serious cyclist, in that I hoped to ride at least four days out of seven, and challenged myself, sometimes by choosing a route that included steep climbs, and almost always by paying attention to my speed. I did my best to maintain a steady, fast cadence, and to keep a good position on the bicycle—let the legs do the work and keep the torso steady, low, and forward, with your hands over the brake hoods. Pedal through the circle, as though you're scraping mud off your foot when you get to the bottom, rather than simply pushing down with one and then the other leg. Get up out of the saddle with your body weight forward when charging up a hill.

I rode alone most of the time. Coming home tired from my office, I knew that changing clothes and getting on the bicycle would be hard to do, so as an incentive I'd promise myself to take it easy and not keep looking at the speedometer. But then, after the first three miles or so, I'd be warmed up and riding hard, easy be damned. On October 1, 2003, my bicycle was in the shop, getting new shifters and brakes. That Wednesday I was worried about a dinner the next day with the trustees and some colleagues, which I had to host as the chair of the faculty. I took that position seriously, perhaps too seriously, because I thought that there was a possibility of creating some kind of pushback to certain of the Wesleyan administration's policies that undermined faculty governance and were demoralizing many of my colleagues. I knew that, starting Thursday evening, October 2, I'd be in meetings and meals for the next three days, so when the bike shop unexpectedly called and said, "It's ready to go," I was delighted. I wasn't going to be moving my body much for the immediate future. The days were getting shorter and the evenings colder.

"Hey, Jake," I said into the phone, "they just called from Pedal Power to tell me that the bike's fixed, so I get to ride today—thank God—because the trustees are in town tomorrow through Saturday dinner. At least I'll get out today, which is great, since they told me it wouldn't be ready before Friday." So when I got home, I tossed my work clothes on the bed, got into cycling gear—including a reflective vest and a helmet—and went out. I imagine I started shifting up as I got to the top of the hill, moving into a higher gear ratio to keep my cadence regular as the climb leveled out. The shifters were new to me that day and shaped differently from my old ones. I was worried about the trustees and my responsibility to my colleagues, as I understood it. Whatever was going on in my head and the rest of my body, I didn't see a branch lying in my way.

The physics of the event are beyond me, but apparently I came to a dead stop when the branch got wedged in the spokes of my front wheel, which pitched the bicycle instantly over to the right.

The force of my full body weight, coupled with the force of violently arrested forward movement, slammed my chin into the pavement. Despite my fast reflexes, my hands were untouched, because it happened too quickly for me to throw them out to break my fall, nor were my shoulders hurt, because I didn't have time to twist my body. The impact of my chin hyperextended my neck so violently that I fractured the fifth and sixth cervical vertebra, which scraped the spinal cord those bones are made to protect. Serious neurological damage started instantly—blood engorged the affected site, and the tissue around the lesion began to swell, causing more and more damage as the cord pressed against the broken vertebrae.

I also smashed my chin into tiny pieces, tore open my lips, slashed open my nose, breaking the cartilage, and multiply fractured the orbital bones underneath my right eye. Since I hit my chin just slightly to the right of center—I must've been reflexively trying to turn my head—the damage runs from that side, through my lips, and across my nose in a diagonal cut. The wire-rim glasses I was wearing were deeply enough embedded in the bridge of my nose to leave a dark half-moon scar that I see in the mirror arching between my eyebrows. Everything bled fiercely, as facial wounds always do, and loss of blood was the most immediate danger. My front teeth were left dangling and one in the lower front was half broken. I didn't lose consciousness—how is that possible?—and was able to tell my name when asked, but nothing else. No, I didn't know what year it was. No, I didn't know who the president was. No, I didn't know where I lived or whom to call. And I had with me no identifying papers of any sort. "I don't feel well. I . . . Don't feel . . . Well," I said, a statement of fact that yielded no useful information.

On one count I was very fortunate. A car was behind, preparing to pass me, when my bicycle pitched sideways so fast that even though the driver had his eye on me, he said he couldn't see what had happened—I just disappeared. The branch caught in a mass of broken spokes told the story. Thankfully, he stopped to help and dialed 911 on his cell phone. When the EMTs arrived, they immediately called the rapid-response helicopter from Hartford Hospital. It landed on the grounds of a graveyard directly across the road from where I lay shattered, bleeding, and unmoving. I imagine a dramatic scene, just at dusk, with lots of flashing lights and whirring helicopter blades. I had left the house wearing my reflective vest just after 6:00, so darkness was coming on fast.

The state trooper who arrived at the scene, Officer Milardo, was left with the task of trying to figure out where I lived. He knew my name, got my address in Middletown, Connecticut, and drove over to the house to see if anyone was there who should know that I was gravely injured and in the emergency room of Hartford Hospital. Friends happen to live directly across the street—when I was in my study I could look over to Anthony's, and he could likewise see mine. He had watched me head off for a ride some time before, so when the cruiser pulled up, he went out to check if something was wrong.

"They're *partners*," Anthony said, gesturing emphatically. "*Partners.*" He was trying to tell the officer whom to call. "She's in New York City, and they're partners," he said, striking the back of his open right hand in the palm of his left for emphasis. So Officer Milardo called Janet in New York City, and reached her in her office at Barnard College. When he identified himself as a state trooper and said, "Are you a friend of Christina Crosby . . . ," she instantly broke in, "How bad? How bad? How bad?" The officer told her that I was in no danger of dying, although I was very seriously hurt. "How are you going to get to Hartford?" "Rent a car," Janet said distractedly, to which he replied, "Take the train. This is no time to drive."

She got onto Metro-North, having called Lori, who lived in New Haven pretty close to the train station. They drove in haste up I-91 to Hartford. Janet had my power of attorney in hand, because she was prepared to do anything to get into the intensive care unit, where only family members are allowed. Imagining me lying there alone . . . she could think only of being by my side. Doug and Midge Bennet, the president of Wesleyan and his wife, were in the waiting room, keeping vigil.

"We've been able to see her. They asked, 'Are you her parents?' and I just lied," Midge said, and Janet was suddenly overcome. Sobbing the first of so many tears, she cried, "I was so afraid, so afraid, no one was here, she was alone." "No, no, we've been by her bed—but you know she's not conscious because she's heavily sedated . . ." At the last, Janet had no need to flourish the power of attorney to come to where I lay motionless, clean, intubated to protect against further swelling that could obstruct my breathing, and quite unconscious.

I was unable to recognize or speak to her until the end of the following day.

3

✳

Bewilderment

How can I give an account of myself after "catastrophic injury"?
That's a technical term used by physicians and insurance companies
for a severe, radically life-changing event like a spinal cord injury. A
chasm—impassable, unbridgeable—opened the instant my chin hit
the pavement, injuring my central nervous system and stranding me
in a violent and unceasing neurological storm. I have no memory
of the minutes leading up to the accident, and the accident itself is
utterly obliterated. I lost days of my life in the ICU—it's only a blur
of fluorescent light. The month that I underwent major surgeries is
lost forever, and the long months in the rehab hospital only gradually
came into focus. Janet reported to friends that I was severely injured
but had suffered no loss of my "personhood." I can't say how happy
that makes me—my face acted as a crumple zone and protected my
brain from injury—but *I* feel alienated, sometimes profoundly alienated, from "myself." My skepticism about my "self" is not only that
of the intellectual taught to be suspicious of such a clearly bounded
rationality, but also an inability to recognize who I have become.

Because of my condition, I've been pondering the reality that everybody has/is a body. Your body emerges through the perception of
others as different from yourself, at a touchable distance, and self-

hood is not self-contained. What you want, who you are, how you feel are all brought into being over time and in relation to others, and those thoughts and feelings are repeatedly inscribed, creating powerful circuits that organize a sense of embodied self. Such is human interdependency that my self-regard depends on your regard for me. I need and want a more fully livable life, which turns importantly, if not exclusively, on this play of recognition.[1] Spinal cord injury has cast me into a surreal neurological wasteland that I traverse day and night. This account is an effort to describe the terrain. I want you to know, and I, myself, want better to understand, a daily venture of living that requires considerable fortitude on my part and a great dependency on others, without whose help my life would be quite literally unlivable.

Whenever you offer an account of yourself to others, you labor to present yourself as coherent and worthy of recognition and attention, as I am doing right now. Yet because my sense of a coherent self has been so deeply affronted, I've also been thinking about stories that are devoted more to affect than to reason, and because the accident and its aftermath were so horrific, horror stories suddenly make sense to me in a way they didn't before. Such stories gather affective intensity as their narratives develop, and often create eerie, uncanny effects by presenting doubles—two where only one should be. Hitchcock uses this device in some of his most famous films. In *Vertigo*, for instance, the story revolves around the emotions of a detective who sees a woman he desires fall to her death while he is paralyzed by vertigo and unable to save her. Then some months later he catches sight of her again, or someone so alike that the resemblance to the dead woman is uncanny. The one he loved seems returned to him, and they begin to date. The uncanny doubling of one woman into two urges doubts that gather into a malevolent uncertainty that haunts their interactions. If she *is* the woman he loved, she's one of the undead dead and must be threatening. If she's *not* the woman he loved, she's playing an elaborate confidence game with him and must be dangerous. But she is so beautiful, and resembles his beloved so strongly, that he finds himself drawn on despite his doubts. A sense of dread increasingly suffuses their interactions.

The childhood in which I was so close to my brother, when we were fiercely competitive and evenly matched, ended in seventh grade, in the junior high where femininity engulfed me. We grew up and grew apart, lovingly enough. He married and went to law school, while I discovered the passions of lesbian feminist practice and politics and went to graduate school. Just as he graduated and was beginning to clerk for a judge, he was diagnosed with MS, and by his late forties was quadriplegic. The contrast in our lives could hardly have been more complete—he was seriously disabled and I was not. In an instant, at the symbolic age of fifty, that contrast collapsed and my childhood fantasy of being his twin seemed malevolently realized, for there we were, each with seriously incapacitating damage to the central nervous system, each in a wheelchair, each requiring intensive assistance just to make it through each day. My brother/myself. Is quadriplegia doubled a fantastic coincidence or foreboding sign? If I am myself, what the hell/who the hell is this body!? My life feels split in two. The horror, the horror.

Spinal cord injury has undone my body, bewildering me and thwarting my understanding. Yet I am certain about one thing— whatever chance I have at a good life, in all senses of that phrase, depends on my openness to the undoing wrought by spinal cord injury, because there is no return to an earlier life. I know that the life I live now depends on my day-by-day relations with others, as it did before, but to an incalculably greater extent. Now I need you to know from the inside, as it were, how it feels to be so radically changed. If I can show you, perhaps I'll be able to see, too. The intricacies of bodymind interactions defy certainties and confound representation, but I see no other way to go on—how else will I understand? How will you?

4

✳

Falling
into Hell

Because I was so powerfully and thankfully drugged, the three weeks that I spent in Hartford Hospital are a jumble of disconnected impressions. The neurosurgeons and the plastic surgeons debated who should go first. My face would remain workable only so long before starting to set, yet my neck was unstable, and needed to be shored up with bone taken from my hip and installed on either side of the fractured vertebrae, or I stood the risk of further damage to the spinal cord. I was in no way conscious of these discussions. Janet was, although the conversation was really among the physicians. The plastic surgeons operated first, and then sent me back to the intensive care unit from which I'd come.

Coming to consciousness, I felt an obstruction in my throat, the tube that prevented me from choking on my tongue. Although its purpose is to allow you to breathe, it felt as though I couldn't, and I remember struggling against it in my mind. When the neurosurgeons put me under, I was once again intubated, only this time when I returned to consciousness my mouth and throat were filled with mucus. I drew each breath through that thick fluid, which seemed to be drowning me. Janet watched over me, using a kind of vacuum tube to suction out some of the goop gurgling in my throat.

These were experiences of powerful discomfort and fear more than of pain, since I was so out of it. Because I had to recover after each surgery, I was in Hartford Hospital for a bit more than three weeks, able to talk, more or less, when I was awake, only a few hours a day. I have a jumbled recollection of being told I had broken my neck and might be paralyzed, or perhaps not—the MRI showed the damage to the spinal cord clearly enough, but there was no knowing what kind of damage it actually had sustained until the swelling began to abate, and that takes a long time. Because Janet was by my side every day, I had the security of her love, which mitigated my fears for the future. I didn't really understand much of what I was being told.

I recall as a kind of dream seeing the stunningly white brightness of an operating room one time as I was being wheeled in. I know that dear friends came to visit me. I know that one day my bowels let loose and I fouled the sheets with liquid waste. I know that I went from the ICU, to the operating room, to the ICU, and then to a "step down" unit, only to return to the operating room and repeat the sequence. My mouth was full of metal, arch bars that ran from side to side to keep the roof of my mouth from caving in—somehow the bits of bone that had been my chin were pinned together, as were other bones in my face—and I wore a very high, tight, and rigid cervical collar around my neck. I could not turn my body or sit up. I could not move my legs or feet. I could not lift my arms or use my hands, which were uselessly curled up into loose fists by atrophying muscles and tightening ligaments.

Right before I was to be discharged to the rehab hospital, orderlies appeared to wheel me away through the corridors, and I watched the labyrinthine greenish ceilings and walls pass by. I was headed for the first of two procedures ("minor surgeries"). The first put a Greenfield filter just at my crotch, in the big vein coming up from my leg, there to catch blood clots that develop when circulation is compromised.

For the second, a surgeon ran a gastrointestinal tube through my abdominal wall and into my stomach so as to pump food into me—I had been on IVs for a month, but when I got to the rehab hospital that would change. When at last I was released from Hartford Hospital, I was delivered by ambulance to the Hospital for Special Care about thirty minutes away. October was nearly over, and I was to stay at HSC until early March. It was there that I knew I was in pain.

* * *

I had been living on an IV drip, ingesting all the while a remarkable quantity of narcotic drugs that slow down the body's systems, and now I was being fed through the GI tube. Every night I was hooked up to a machine that forced puréed food into my stomach, so I imperatively had to begin moving my bowels. Thus the horror of gastrointestinal gas began, which left my skin savagely tight over my distended abdomen. Although I was being given NuLytely, a mightily powerful drug used to empty bowels—you may have used it when cleaning yourself out before a colonoscopy—I could not relieve myself. You're quickly in big trouble if you're not moving waste from your body. As I learned, "bowels lead," a simple truth with profound ramifications. Constipation, uncomfortable for anyone, is a real threat when emerging from surgery, because the body recovers from general anesthesia slowly. I had been under twice, and each time for a long time.

The doctors needed to know whether there was a bowel obstruction, which raised the specter of another surgery. I was therefore transferred out of my bed onto a stretcher and wheeled through this new hospital, into a big stainless steel box of an elevator, and down to the radiology unit. In a dark and cold room, a technician prepared to do a sonogram of my poor abdomen. When she began spreading the gel on me, I begged her to stop—It burns! It burns! It burned because the gel was cool, and I was so neurologically scrambled that cool felt hot on my belly. How was I to describe this pain, lost in a body so foreign to me I could translate it into speech only in the most primitive way? The gas I understood, because my gastrointestinal tract has always gone awry when I'm under stress. I suffered terrible car sickness when I was a kid, and later on in college lived with acid indigestion I treated with Rolaids from a great big jar I kept on my desk. As an adult, I'd experienced gas pains that at times left me doubled over. Nothing, however, prepared me for the experience of intestinal gas so high and so impossible to pass. I literally could not fart. All below my rib cage was more or less paralyzed, increasingly so as you moved down my body and that included, of course, my bowels, my rectum, my anus. So I was turned on my side, and Winnie, my kind, thoughtful, and skillful nurse, inserted into me a tube with a plastic bag on the end that would inflate if gas passed out of me. Maggie, who day after day sat with me, reports that one time when suffering this way I said, "Winnie, the pain in my intestine is coming from my unconscious." Doubtless I was at least partly right. No surprise, your unconscious awaits as you begin to recover from catastrophic injury.

I was plagued with thirst. The arch bars in my mouth and the pins in my face were causing the muscles in my face and throat to atrophy. The bones in my face were still unstable, the many tiny parts not yet fused with the pins. I couldn't swallow water, although I could manage a thicker liquid like yogurt. Nor could I keep my mouth closed. My lower lip had been split open, and even now does not completely close to make a seal with my upper—I hold my lips together with my hand when I rinse with mouthwash. At the time, I understood nothing of this. All I knew is that night after night after night I would awake with a raging thirst. That phrase, raging thirst, is a cliché only because when you are really thirsty, your need for water feels so exigent that the thirst holds you hostage, loudly raging for water, water, water. Water. Water. Please, water. My mouth was so terribly dry. The whole of my being felt desperate with thirst. When a CNA would appear in response to my call, she would fill a small paper cup with ice water and immerse a little green sponge on the end of a wooden stick, then put the wet sponge in my mouth. I would suck at it. The cold water felt so good, but I got just a tiny amount, and would ask for more. More, please, more. Are you done, the aide would ask. No. Another, please. Please. But she was pressed for time, and would move away, and I would close my eyes and try despairingly to breathe through my nose, feeling my lips begin to part all the while.

Late at night, as the earth turned toward the small hours, when I was wrenched from sleep by my thirst, I would awake on a wholly different floor, somewhere upstairs in the hospital—so I thought in my confusion. There I was cared for by a beneficent Polish woman in her later middle age who helped me when I called, on fire. She would fill the cup and give me the icy, wet sponge, again, yet again, yes, please, yes. Finally, smiling kindly, she would turn the small paper cup upside down. "All gone, you drank it all!" She would fill it again and stay with me until I said, "Enough, thank you." I am uncertain of her name (Elizabeth?), but will be forever grateful for her compassion.

More dreadful than the gas or the gel, even more terrible than the terrible thirst, were the painful currents running through my body. I'd never felt anything remotely like it. My drugged sleep yielded up a vivid nightmare—my skeleton was burning, every bone outlined in red. Pain felt like electricity somehow let loose on me, a statement that is both figurative and not, because the signal that passes biochemically from one neuron to another, lighting up neural networks, is, in fact, electrical—the passage of ions down the axon of a neuron and across the synapse to another neuron, continually, instantly accomplished trillions of times in complex networks all through your body. Trillions. My central nervous system was sending out solar flares. Perhaps the most terrible night came weeks into my stay at the Hospital for Special Care, when I finally grasped the extent of my paralysis. I awoke at night on fire, my skin crisping from the soles of my feet, up my legs and back, tight around my abdomen right up to just under my rib cage, and down my arms onto my hands. I was burning the way you burn when shocked with static electricity, but the shock was infinitely multiplied and running thickly, continuously under my skin. This ferocious buzzing was let loose on me by scrambled nerves that will never ever fully recover, neurological pain that could outline my body by thickly fizzing my skin, as it did that night, or more deeply penetrate my extremities, as was sometimes the case. What a horror, to finally and viscerally understand how profoundly I was hurt! I "knew," of course, from bedside conversations with my physicians and with Janet all that was known about the injury I had sustained. My mind was intact, but how could I understand a body so fundamentally transformed? I had no real idea until then of the *scope* of my injury, how far up on my body it came. And what a horror that the drugs I was being given didn't make it stop!

It called to mind another hospital. I was seven years old and having a tonsillectomy. On my back in the operating room, I looked up at the gowned and gloved adults who were looking down at me. "Count backwards from one hundred," I was instructed, as a mask hissing ether was put over my nose and mouth. Then in the seconds it took for me to lose consciousness I felt myself falling free, nauseated and gassed, through black space dotted all over with points of colored light. I clearly saw myself, outlined as if by a gingerbread cookie cutter, plummeting down, down. I was, for those seconds, sure I was going to hell.

Now I was there.

*   *   *

Years after my discharge from the Hospital for Special Care, there's no discernible pattern that I can see to account for the good nights and bad nights. Most often I lie on my side, having positioned my legs so that the top one is drawn up, bent at the knee with my foot resting on a pillow so that the bony protrusion of my bunion, where thin skin stretches tightly over bone, does not touch the sheet and begin to throb. (Bunions, I've learned, are big toes that have been drawn in toward the smaller ones so that the joint on the side of the foot sticks out, making it wider at that point. These malformations developed as the ligaments and tendons of my foot contracted, which has also given me hammer toes.) After arranging my foot, I lie down and put one hand under the pillow, palm up and fingers spread, so that the weight of my head will stretch it open. So positioned, now and then I realize to my surprise that the electricity has been turned off and I'm not in pain. Unless I consciously try to move my legs, they're just there. I can feel the weight of the duvet, and feel that one leg is bent, the other straight— though just where each leg rests on the sheet can get confusing. I lie there quietly.

More often than not I feel myself buzzing. Eleven years after the accident, on good days, pain recedes into the background of life, and when I'm outwardly engaged I don't think about the fact that I almost always feel a current running through my body. Yet sometimes I can't ignore the pain, when my skin feels thick, electrified, and vibrating. You can imagine a wet suit, the kind you'd use when windsurfing. I had one—it was made of neoprene that hugged my body tightly, and when wet held next to my skin a thin layer of water warmed by my body heat. My skin feels like that neoprene, thick and pliable, with an electric current carried through the underside wetness of blood and lymph. At this very moment of writing, I feel that current making a bold outline of my body. My feet and ankles (which swell, sometimes prodigiously, over the course of the day) buzz all the way through, while my thighs and sit bones press uncomfortably against the seat. My fingers are cold, thick, and buzzing, and stay cold unless the temperature's above 80°. This phenomenon plagues me because the injury to my spinal cord is right at the level where the spinal nerves connecting my hands to my brain branch out between the vertebrae, and those neural networks are implacably compromised. There was a pharmacologist on the staff of the rehab hospital who had a round, white button pinned on the lapel of his lab coat—PAIN was spelled out in red letters, with the international "forbidden" line in black drawn diagonally through the word from upper right to lower left. My chronic neurological pain gave the lie to that button by insistently breaching that line when I was in the hospital, and continues—though moderated—to break through whatever drug is on offer.

Sometimes the buzzing is more like burning, so that my skin feels like crinkly hot Saran wrap. That's what happened last night. It reminded me of just how horrible I felt in the hospital, and how long I felt horrible, when I wondered in rehab whether I would ever be free of that pain. Most of the time, pain only seeps through the narcotic and other chemical barriers set against it, yet it still can feel terrifying, not necessarily in the moment, but as a fated repetition. Sometimes at night I wake to it, and sometimes I fall asleep, drugged, in it. Sometimes the burning is accompanied by spasticity, as my left leg—or my right one—begins to stiffen and shake for a few seconds, and then relax, but relax for less than a minute, only to go into another spasm. The spasticity itself comes in waves: cramping, quivering, jumping, jerking my leg so that there is no sleep for me—or for Janet—without further pharmacological intervention. So I take a

Valium, and lie there in bed, thinking about embodied life until I'm knocked out.

Coldness has pursued me from the first, in the hospital where Janet would find me in my overheated room, lying in bed, freezing. She would warm up flannel sheets in the clothes dryer down the hall, three at a time, and wrap me up in them. The warmth was wonderfully soothing, but so wretchedly transient, because the coldness emerges from deep within my body. I have long since left the hospital, but my circulation will always be impaired, my nerves damaged, and my hands cold.

If only pain could be vanquished. It is inescapable, unless you resort to illegal drugs, and even then pain waits on the other side. The cocktail of drugs against pain that I was given in the Hospital for Special Care included OxyContin, the artificial opiate that's like heroin, only made in a lab rather than derived from opium poppies grown in Afghanistan. Now on the streets it's often preferred to heroin—it's uniform in effect and less likely to kill you. One time, and one time only, OxyContin was put into my body pulverized along with all my other drugs, which were given to me nightly through the gastrointestinal tube. As always during that time, I was in pain, cold, and desperate for some relief. Lying there, I felt a soothing warmth coursing through my body, warm honey in my veins, which spread and spread, engulfing me. So sweet. How unspeakably *lovely* are these drugs!—a thought I held onto for maybe fifteen minutes, floating along before sleep took me. If only I could take my OxyContin that way always! My mind was relieved from the fear that I would always be in pain, and when I'm buzzing, cold, or burning, I sometimes remember the sensation of being warmed through and suspended in no-pain, weightless. Then I long to be taken out of myself and the pain that plagues me, as I was that one time. If I were to crush and swallow my OxyContin tablets, pain would give way to a surplus of pleasure, sweetly running all through my body toward oblivion. I would drift away. Nodding off on OxyContin would, of course, in the end make my pain fatally unbearable. OxyContin is an extended-release formulation of the narcotic. If I crushed the tablets I would get a concentrated hour of bliss. But I would have used in an hour a dose meant for twelve, so I've never crushed a tablet, and they all remain whole in the pill organizer. As a result, I am almost never completely pain free.

Pain brings with it a dour companion, loneliness. I feel an un-assuageable loneliness, because I will never be able to adequately describe the pain I suffer, nor can anyone accompany me into the realm of pain. I've learned that the recourse to analogy is not solely mine, since pain is so singular that it evades direct description, so isolating because in your body alone. Crying, and screaming, and raging against pain are the sign of language undone.[1] "As if" is pain's rhetorical signature, which requires the displacement of metaphor to signify—its properties can be articulated only by way of something else, and the tropes of pain display the awkwardness of catachresis. My electrified neoprene skin holds me in its tight, suffusing embrace. The current races close to the surface, yet somehow also deeply penetrates the tissue. My fingers fumble. My toes curl upward.

If you went to the doctor's office complaining of pain, you would be asked first to rank it, on a scale of 1 to 10. There is a chart, exactly the same everywhere, showing faces as emoticons—a smiling face, with an upward curving line for the mouth, dots for eyes, with happy eyebrows drawn above—that's 1, feeling no pain. Ten, by contrast, has a sharply downturned mouth, pinched eyebrows, and dot eyes leaking tears. When I complained of pain in the hospital, the nurse invariably asked me to rate it on that 1–10 scale, an exercise I found quite confusing—the night of fiery, engirdling pain was the worst I'd suffered, so for a while any other pain felt relatively trivial. I would be buzzing and intolerably cold, but would only say, "5 or maybe 6." That ranking yielded but one short-acting dose of oxycodone. Even though giving my pain a higher number could get me two, I was afraid of ranking it too high, for fear of not being able to go high enough when it got excruciating.

Before too long, however, my rankings crept upward, and I would ask for as much narcotic help as I could get, with inevitable side effects. I would fall asleep in the middle of speaking a sentence. It was January, and Lori had just returned from her motorcycle tour of New Zealand, by lesbians, for lesbians—we had talked excitedly together about this adventure in the summer of 2003, when I had the Triumph and she was riding a Kawasaki. She had taken ravishing photographs of the landscape, plus some great pictures of the bikes. I wanted to know about it all, but I struggled, frustrated and help-less, against a kind of narcotic narcolepsy. Yet I wanted those drugs. My bowels, already a great trouble to me since they're slowed by paralysis, had an even harder time moving—but that didn't matter. When electricity stormed through my body, I just wanted relief. The hardest part was waiting in pain after I pushed the button on my call bell. A CNA would eventually show up to ask what I needed, and then she had to find a nurse with access to the locked-down drugs. The nurse inevitably would be working with someone else, and there was nothing to do but wait. When I suffered at the time of a shift change, I knew that I'd have to be patient. Moreover, HSC was routinely understaffed, as are all hospitals now. I learned to rank my pain quite high and to request all the meds that I could get, side effects be damned.

In the years just before I broke my neck, I was deeply happy. I was joyfully engaged with my lover, delighting in her body and my own. One afternoon together, we discovered an anatomy book in a downtown Tucson store with a miscellaneous stock—toys for kids, funky sunglasses, witty postcards, and suchlike. Among the stuff was an illustrated book anatomizing the human body, with lovely simplified drawings of the viscera, the skin, the spinal cord, the fiber of nerves coated with myelin, ball and socket joints, the skeleton, blue veins and red arteries, the heart with its four chambers, sexual organs with the hydraulic apparatuses clearly detailed. Lying in bed, we would look at this book and consider the myriad pleasures of the flesh. Embodied life was then an affirmation of fully realized pleasures integrated with a rich intellectual life. One evening, when we lay side by side, reading, I repeatedly interrupted her to exclaim about some sentence in my book, *The Volatile Body*, by the philosopher Elizabeth Grosz.[2] I'll always remember the warm, dry desert air, the lamplight, our proximity, and the book, because then the question of how to represent embodiment was a question of pleasure, first and foremost, and of the mysterious way language could amplify that pleasure. Now, representing bodily sensations is no longer a matter of finding words for the ever renewable resource of shared sexual pleasures, but of finding words for the beyond, the nowhere of pain that I suffer alone.

Janet takes exception to that last sentence, observing that, while she can't feel in her body what I feel in mine, my pain does affect her. She is pained by my suffering—she so wishes it were different, and her desire to make it so is baffled. She's right. Pain does radiate out into the social world, because it changes the person who feels the bodily pain, which in turn cannot but affect those to whom she relates. I have no exact account of how pain changes my interactions with my students and my colleagues, but I know there are times when I don't feel fully present. It's not that the pain is so bad that it commands all my attention, but rather that it's so chronic as to act like a kind of screen. I don't talk much about the pain to anybody other than my therapist, who is not my lover, or my friend, or a member of my family, or my colleague. To her I will complain bitterly, but not to others. I won't complain about the pain because such plaints become corrosive, and would eat at the ties that bind me to others. It's not that I'm bravely suffering in silence, but rather that I know there's nothing to be done.

5

✳

Caring at
the Cash Nexus

"Ah Goddamn it—Jesus Christ, Jesus Christ . . ." I moaned and cursed the pain electrifying my body as I lay in my bed at the Hospital for Special Care. A CNA was by my side, and when I glanced up, I saw a small gold cross on a delicate chain around her neck. Miserable as I was, I thought that I must have offended her sensibilities, and apologized. Her voice was quiet and gentle. "You couldn't have called on a better name."

This simple affirmation of her faith relieved me of embarrassment, for Donna transfigured my oath into praise for her Lord. I decided then and there it would be better for me to stop swearing in company, reserving oaths and obscenities for my private relief. I now say "gosh," "heck," "darn," "goodness," the acceptable refuges of offensive language, and those words no longer feel foreign in my mouth. The only time that I really let loose as I used to do is when I'm alone and have dropped something for the fifth time, or have spilled something, or am troubled with a spasm, or the dog has made a mess—then my language is as foul as it ever was. Moxie Doxie, our alert little dog, doesn't know I'm taking the Lord's name in vain.

When Janet and I were trying to prepare ourselves for my return to our home, we were simply overwhelmed. I'd been hospitalized and under the care of aides, nurses, therapists, and physicians for more than five months, and the thought of managing my care alone was terrifying. Friends were an invaluable help, but I honestly don't know how we could've managed that first week or the ones that followed without the help of a CNA. We needed someone to put on the compression boots and elevate my legs, bring me breakfast and feed it to me, and help me with the wretchedly painful work of stretching out ligaments, tendons, and muscles that had atrophied. We needed help getting me to a tub, because our only bathroom was on the second floor. Janet had gotten installed a chair that ran on a rail up the side of the stairs so that I could get up there, but my arrival felt like an epic achievement, every time. To get me to the tub and shower me, Donna had to transfer me (1) from the bed onto my wheelchair, (2) from the wheelchair onto the stair-lift chair that would take me upstairs, (3) off it and onto a folding wheelchair that was stored in a closet outside the bathroom, (4) from that wheelchair onto the shower bench straddling the toilet and the tub, and (5) finally onto the shower chair (like a commode, but without the bowl) in the tub itself. She and Janet together held me upright, played the water over me, washed my hair and my body, and then reversed all those steps to take me back to bed—without Donna to do those ten transfers, helped by Janet, I would have had sponge baths for months and months. Donna had been a steady, sure, skilled help to me, working the second shift every weekend of my long months at the Hospital for Special Care. I knew that I felt comfortable with her. Her mother had died right around the time that I broke my neck, so as I was crying over my broken body and upended life, she was in the first flood of deep, deep grief for her mother. We were both in mourning. Sometimes we talked, more often we were silent, and both were okay. So I asked, will you come to Middletown and work for me 8:00–12:30, Monday through Friday? To my enormous relief, she said yes.

* * *

Donna still cares for me, and will continue to far into the future, if I continue fortunate. I love her, and she loves me, for a decade of intimate care has created an intimate bond. We've talked about a world of things. She knows that I'm not a church-going Christian, though I come from a Christian family, and I've told her directly that I respect her religious faith and religious practices. I've told her lots of stories about my family life, and have gone on at some length about the evils of capitalism as we know it. She understands that Janet has become the chief executive officer of our home, and goes to her when medical supplies need to be replenished—indeed, when any household matter needs to be addressed. She knows me, what I can—and, as importantly, can't—do. She knows a lot about my relationship with Janet and the terms in which we understand ourselves.

For my part, I know that Donna is a Pentecostal Protestant and has had the life-transforming experience of being saved. She actively studies the Bible and regularly attends the church to which her mother took her five children every Sunday. I know that her loving mother moved those children to Hartford from Brooklyn after her husband was robbed and shot dead in his cab. Donna was six years old. I know how hard Donna has worked to rear well her daughter and son, and now Kyla has graduated from college and Tyler has graduated from high school. I know that she looks to God every day—every hour—for help, and the gospels that she hums as she works suggest that her mind is often on her Savior. I know in a way that I never could have learned otherwise than through such an intimate relationship how bitterly, sometimes desperately, hard it is to be working poor. To have only the change from a twenty that you broke when you got gas, and you have yet to get groceries. To be indentured to the used car dealer who will sell to you even when you have lousy credit, only to trap you in a debt with compounding interest that will continue to demand repayment long after the car has been towed away.

Donna works harder than anyone else I've ever known, and still has constant, nagging, impossible-to-forget worries about upcoming bills. She picks up extra shifts at the hospital all the time, even as she is working a second job for me. She works "doubles," sixteen hours straight through. Yet the bills keep coming. We've talked about how easy it is to get a "payday loan"—just google the phrase and you can see for yourself. Online or in person, the application takes but a moment, and will screw you for years. Check out CashAdvance.com. Here's what you'll learn about interest rates if you scroll down, down the page past the many smiling faces to the small print:

> The APR on a short term loan can range *from 200% to 2,290%* depending on how the APR is calculated (nominal vs. effective), the duration of the loan, loan fees incurred, late payment fees, non-payment fees, loan renewal actions, and other factors. Keep in mind that the APR range is not your finance charge and your *finance charge will be disclosed later on.* [my emphasis throughout]

CNA work is hard and low wage, which means that in Connecticut and New York City many of the workers are African Americans or Caribbean immigrants, though here in central Connecticut, the working class also includes many immigrant Poles and Latin@s. Most patients in a rehab hospital are unable to stand without assistance, let alone walk. Many are simply dead weight. Aides must transfer them from bed to wheelchair and wheelchair to bed several times a day, and help people on and off the toilet, all day long. They have to lift and turn patients in bed, a task that will simply kill your back if you don't do it right. CNAs everywhere now work short staffed as a matter of course—it's called "enhanced productivity." While profits as bright and light as digital numbers flow upward, bodies remain intransigently heavy. Donna's in her early forties. She has a bulging disc in her neck, which radiates pain, and a knee badly in need of replacement. Frequent headaches are just a fact of life. Not a day passes without pain, though some days are worse than others. I'll see her put a hand to her back or rub her neck, involuntary gestures that announce she's hurting, and now and then she walks with a pronounced limp. Her doctor advises her to wait for surgery until she absolutely can't stand the knee pain, because a mechanical joint lasts only fifteen to twenty years. Artificial joints wear out like the body parts they replace, and eventually the replacement has to be replaced, so best to push back the first operation as long as possible. Working in the hospital is also highly stressful. Short staffing requires that the CNAs on the job always have patients *waiting* for care, with their call lights reproachfully blinking. Aides and nurses are always behind. Donna keeps her responsibilities alive in her head, which is great for me—she remembers my schedule even when I don't, and anticipates what I need. In the hospital, however, that organizational capacity of hers is wearing, because while she's helping one person, she'll have in mind the woman who needs to get from her bed to the toilet, the other woman who asked for pain medication, and the paralyzed man with a bedsore who has to be turned right on schedule, right *now*. That's high-stress work, and a very hard way to make a living.

I've read that certain populations in our country are given over to "slow death," among them workers in the bottom-level jobs of the one reliably expanding industry in the United States, healthcare.[1] The business section of the *New York Times* reports that "personal care aides will make up the fastest-growing occupation this decade[, and an] Economic Policy Institute study found that some 57 percent of them live in poverty."[2] That phrase, "slow death," captures the endless process of wearing down, the enervating demand of small yet consequential decisions (Can I bring takeout home for the kids tonight? How much can I pay on the electric bill so they don't shut it off?), and the quiet despair that can suffuse everyday life. Wellness programs, like the one directed at CNAs at the Hospital for Special Care, are just another reason to feel bad about yourself—why aren't you going to the gym, with weight machines and elliptical machines and a heated pool, just waiting for you? Regular exercise, moreover, is just the beginning of what's required for a healthy body. With Michelle Obama's bright encouragement, you know you have only yourself to blame for making poor "choices" that undermine your family's health, starting with decisions about food. Such decisions, however, can be imagined to be those of an autonomous and freely willing subject only if you abstract the embodied realities of grinding poverty into weightless ideas—it's called "grinding" precisely because it wears you down and wears you out.

I smoked cigarettes in college, but gave it up years ago. No one I know at Wesleyan still smokes, though when I came in 1982 I could always bum a cigarette at a party. Now the people who smoke are the ones working low-wage, high-stress, physically demanding jobs. People smoke in order to take a break and hang out in the parking lot with their friends, and they smoke to schedule in the sharp pleasure of doing what their bodies desire in an otherwise dreary and repetitive day.[3] Coke delivers caffeine and a much-needed sugar kick that feels good in the moment. Fried food tastes right and at McDonald's reliably will taste right every time. You can pick it up at the drive-through and eat it in your car driving to your second job. If you look at the advertisements on daytime TV, you'll see (1) personal injury lawyers asking if you've been injured at work, and (2) diets organized around prepackaged food that costs a lot just because it's prepackaged, and (3) smoking-cessation programs. You may be on your couch watching daytime TV because you were hurt on the job, but you could, nonetheless, lose weight and quit smoking. You could make healthy choices—if you don't, it's your own damn fault.

* * *

I know a lot about Donna, yet her life remains, in many regards, unknown to me and unknowable. She works *for* me, in *my* home, and has to learn *my* ways and the ways of *my* household. It's just a fact that black people know "the ways of white folk," in Langston Hughes's turn of phrase.[4] Black people in this country have been taking care of white people in their homes as domestic workers for centuries, necessarily amassing many generations of knowledge about the oddities of how white people live. I listen to arias from Baroque operas that were written for castrati who sang in the soprano range, music now performed by countertenors, who are men singing in falsetto. How bizarre is that? Neither I nor the white women who are my colleagues will be taking jobs in the homes of black women, and getting to know their lives as only a caretaker can—intimately, every day, over time. *Of course* Donna knows more about me than I know about her. I know that we depend on each other. Our mutual dependence does not, however, bring me into her household, and there's plenty I don't know about her life, despite our personal closeness.

To rebuild our lives after my terrible accident, Janet and I turned to our families and friends. Their financial support made so much possible that otherwise would have simply been out of reach that first terrible year, and I continue to be actively thankful for their open-handed generosity. We've told Donna that if there's ever a crisis she can come to us, and forgo the payday loan. Borrowing from us, she would be spared onerous interest rates. We can get our hands on money. She can't. Our good intentions, however, can't transcend the structural racism that has advantaged us so grandly, and disadvantaged her so wrongly. I am seriously worried about patronage, for which there are all too many precedents. The black artists of the Harlem Renaissance, including Langston Hughes, were patronized by well-off "white folks" who supported "their" authors, facilitated the production of "their" artists' books, and then took the privilege money afforded them to suggest how "their" artists should go about their lives. What if Janet or I somehow patronize Donna? The prospect makes me ill. My delicate feelings, however, are no guarantee against patronage—our intimacy is very real, but it's we who have the money.

There's a constitutional amendment forbidding slavery, and indentured servitude has long since been a thing of the past, but as of the early twenty-first century, white people with money too often still do not honor the workers who labor in their homes or compensate them fairly. Were wages calculated on a different scale, according to how dearly loved are those in need of care, domestic labor would no longer come so cheap! Righteous anger may be some relief, but there's no ethically safe solution for me, or for any employer of caring labor. Political action is the only effective response to systematic injustice. My contribution as an educator has been teaching *Valuing Domestic Work*, the fifth in the Barnard Center for Research on Women's series New Feminist Solutions.[5] It's a report "based on a three-year collaboration with Domestic Workers United (DWU) and the National Domestic Workers Alliance (NDWA)," which lays out the political groundwork required for transformative action. I don't confuse putting this report on my syllabus with the work of organizing. Teaching the report is instead a way to name social reproduction as an object of knowledge consequential to feminist thought, and to link my dependency to a broader vision of caring labor and reproductive work. It is to see the political in the personal and the personal in the political.

I must simply admit, however, that my personal relationship to Donna is an irresolvable contradiction. We meet at the cash nexus, the labor market. Donna brings to that market her bodily capacity for work and her imperative need for money, while I bring money and my imperative need for help with my bodily incapacities. Donna can't live without money, and I am glad to pay her what I owe. Yet money cannot begin to measure the value of her work. Money cannot calculate what Donna's presence does for me or how she goes about the profoundly intimate work of helping me manage my body. *I value her for who she is*, the beautiful, gentle, skillful, kind, sad, singular person that I love.

6

✷

Lost
in Space

By the time I was discharged from Hartford Hospital, I was skeletal. I didn't know that startling fact because I didn't know anything,
really, about my body. Muscle atrophies at an alarming rate, especially when you're on an IV drip of glucose solution for three and a
half weeks. Later, when I was in the Hospital for Special Care, I was
fed through the gastrointestinal tube that snaked from a machine
beside the bed and then disappeared under the covers. I would get
hooked up every night before the lights went out at 9:30, and would
hear a faint hum as puréed goop went through my abdominal wall
into my stomach. I wore a johnnie, of course, when in bed, one of
those curious hospital garments of indifferently printed fabric that
tie behind your back, ensuring hospital personnel easy access to your
body. I intentionally chose not even to try touching my body underneath that fabric, and turned my mind away from my flesh. I was
afraid of the tubes, one putting food into me, the other a catheter
that took urine out. You could see it dripping yellow into the Foley
bag hung on the side of the bed, that big bag necessary to collect the
urine flowing from the catheter inserted into my urethra.

When I would get stripped and then rolled over onto the shower
gurney and wheeled into the shower, I couldn't hold my head up to see

my body. I never asked for a mirror, and when I came upon one now and again in the physical therapy room, I would assiduously look away. Not only was it very difficult, quite literally, for me to see my body, but also I was afraid to know. I had no sense of what all the metal in my mouth was about, vaguely imagining I had braces, since I didn't understand that bars were arched over the roof of my mouth to keep it from collapsing. Nor did I grasp how the plastic surgeons had worked on my face. I have a scar under my chin where, incomprehensibly, the surgeons pulled the skin up—like turning a glove inside out—so as to repair as best they could the shattered bones thus revealed. Grasping the enormity of the injuries that I had suffered was too hard. I could not tell with any exactitude where I was in space. In the first months when I was in the hospital, two aides had to work to position me before lights out, using pillows behind and between my legs to keep me lined up just right. The instructions for this positioning were drawn by my physical therapist and posted on a bulletin board above my bed, and I had been present when Dr. Seetherama discussed with the nurses the importance of so arranging my body to minimize my pain. Janet told me repeatedly all that had happened and was happening to me. I simply could not take it all in. My body was alien to me, and lost in space.

* * *

After a while, when the big cervical brace came off, I could gingerly lift my head off the pillow. I could move my arms back and forth a little. I could not, however, pick anything up, a home truth I learned when Patty, my well-trained and gracefully intuitive occupational therapist, put a Kleenex on the tray in front of me and instructed me to pick it up and move it to the side. She had recently graduated from the University of Hartford, where she had played Division I soccer while studying in the university's strong program for occupational and physical therapies. We developed a good relationship, based in part on my regard for her athletic achievements. When I couldn't even pick up the tissue, I was in despair, crying and saying, "I used to be so strong, I used to be so strong." Saying it again and again. I spoke the truth. I wept and mourned the muscles that had disappeared.

Phenomenologists speak of a body image that is part of our mental equipment, a way of picturing our bodies in space. It's possible, of course, to have a profoundly distorted sense of your body's shape, as do young women afflicted with anorexia, who look at themselves and see fat where others see a skeletal body wrapped in skin. I can't remember not thinking of my body as strong. I grew up in a small town in the 1950s, in rural, mountainous central Pennsylvania. Huntingdon is a largely white working-class town with an Owens Corning fiberglass plant just a couple blocks down Washington Street from my home on Mifflin Street. The main line of the Pennsylvania Railroad runs through Huntingdon, passing just three and a half blocks to the west of Mifflin. There's a handsome railroad station building downtown, but it stands empty and unused—these days only one passenger train a day going east stops at Huntingdon, and one going west. I guess you pay for your ticket when you get on board. A small number of black people were concentrated through the default segregation of real estate in a neighborhood at the very edge of the town, between Stone Creek and Route 22, so my world was very white. The immediate neighborhood of my childhood mixed economic classes together pretty indiscriminately, though, and all the kids played together. My brother, Jeff, and I were told only that we lived a very privileged life, and that it was our responsibility to be considerate of the "underprivileged," a category that remained compelling, but vague.

In our neighborhood, I always played games with the boys, and my brother and I would roughhouse all the day long. Being a "tomboy" brought with it various confusions and insults, but the truth is that I couldn't imagine playing girls' games, and was skilled enough, strong enough, and fast enough to play with the boys. One summer my father taught both Jeff and me how to throw a baseball, pivoting so that the torque of the whole body goes into the pitch. We were playing pitch and catch in the dirt road by our campsite in a state park when Jeff's hard-thrown baseball smacked into the webbing of my glove. I stepped into my return, and the trajectory of my pitch was flat, too. "That's it," Dad shouted. So I never "threw like a girl," nor did I ever run with my elbows out, hands held up and away from my body, as so many girls somehow learned to do.

I was proud of my strength and my coordination, and played hard. Huntingdon was surrounded by fields in the valley bottoms and woods running up the long mountain ridges, and was truly rural just beyond the town borders. The Juniata River had carved through rock over many millennia, creating "the cliffs," rocks jutting out into empty space with a sheer drop-off down to the railroad tracks and river. When we were kids, Mother would some evenings pack a picnic supper into a wicker basket, and get us into the car. Dad would drive up Taylor Highlands. Jeff and I, always competing, would "horsengoggle" to see who got to be "the pathfinder," and with either him or me in the vanguard, we would walk out to the flat-topped cliffs and the spectacular view. To get there, you had to pass under huge power lines that hummed and crackled as the wires on their high towers ran off into the distance, the ground beneath filled with brambles and bushes—mountain laurel, and sometimes thickets of blueberries and blackberries entangled with other greenery. Heat shimmered over the brush and rocks, and it smelled like summer. The pathfinder got to choose which rock we would picnic on, and while Mother unpacked our food and drink, Jeff and I would vie to be the first to "I spy" a freight train coming around the bend in the distance, hauling a mile of coal cars—and get too close to the edge for parental comfort. So Dad looped two ropes around his hand, the other ends of which were passed through the belt buckles of our shorts.

When I was older, I climbed all over the cliffs, and hiked up the power line with my army surplus canteen strapped on my belt. I rode my bicycle for miles, in town when I was young, and out into the country when I got older. I climbed trees, lots of trees, hanging upside down by my knees, then scrambling higher and higher. One sunny and breezy June day when I was ten or eleven years old, I got far up in a tall evergreen tree near the edge of a small woods overlooking the college science center. The sap on the trunk was sweet and dark, and my hands got more and more sticky as I went from limb to limb, repeatedly catching my T-shirt on small branches as I continued to climb. I got as high as I could, until the tree bowed under my weight and swayed in the wind. Leaning far into the air under a blazingly blue sky, I heard the breeze soughing through the stand of pines, and breathed in the hot summer smell of pine tar. When I was a teenager, my friends and I would drive out of town a couple miles, park by the side of the road and walk through the woods to Stone Creek, where we knew about a small swimming hole. Jeans and work shirts piled up next to sneakers and boots. Up on Taylor Highlands there was an old water tower hidden away at the end of a road that petered off into gravel ruts overrun with weeds. Around the tower ran a chain-link fence with a rusty padlock on the gate. I would go by myself, climb over the fence, taking care not to catch myself on the top, and drop down to the other side. Then up the skinny metal ladder that turned sharply vertical at the top, making me feel as if I were somehow climbing upside down for that last section, just below the little metal grate of the runway platform that went around the tank. Up there you could see out over the town to the mountain ridges running off into the distance. Up there you could feel the wind pick up as a storm was coming in. Up there I was trespassing, and I loved it.

That childhood world is long ago and far away, yet my memory is green, in part, I'm sure, because I took with me into adult life a love of play and pleasure in physical challenges. I would arm wrestle with anybody, and especially loved occasionally besting men. By the time I reached my fiftieth year, I was proud to the point of vanity of the well-defined muscles that had come naturally to me, so to speak, a genetic inheritance from my dad, in part, and the rest the result of all that play, from kick the can in the backyard to varsity sports in high school and college. After I graduated from Swarthmore in the mid-seventies, I took to running when I got home from work, first in my sneakers, and then in the running shoes that had just started being marketed to people like me.

And I always had a bike. My first year out of college, I rode a nine-mile round-trip to my workplace, which solved the problem of gridlock during D.C. rush hour, and as a graduate student in Providence, I bicycled everywhere for years. I started going to New York City in 2000, when Janet began working as the director of the Barnard Center for Research on Women. Unsurprisingly, I learned that cycling was the fastest way to get around Manhattan, faster even then the subway, unless you got really lucky and caught the express from the 96th Street station. I loved riding up 6th Avenue at night, holding my place in the yellow stream of cabs as traffic surged onto Central Park South, past the horses and carriages lined up waiting for fares, around Columbus Circle, swinging at last onto the relative calm of Central Park West.

I'd always bought used bikes, but when bone spurs put an end to my running at age forty, I purchased my first new one since my childhood. I did so in consultation with my friend John. He was a dear friend of my then lover, Elizabeth, and I discovered in graduate school what a great playmate he was. The three of us often took bicycle rides on the beautiful back roads of Connecticut. He rode a German bicycle, built for speed, with narrow tires and clip-in pedals designed to secure cycling shoes with cleats. When he finally persuaded me to buy a really good road bike, he went with me to his bicycle store, where I was fitted for a beautiful Schwinn that was at the low end of the high-tech, high-price machines. I sat on a bicycle in a stand while the sales clerk ran his measuring tape down my legs and over my arms. When I picked up my new machine I was dazzled by its brilliance: silver aluminum, light weight, and it fit me perfectly. I called it the Silver Streak. I had cycling shorts, with the proper padding to ease sitting on the narrow saddle, and loved how tight they were, how they showed off my quads, hamstrings, and glutes.

Phenomenologists talk about a "felt sense" of the body, a schema that emerges from the desire that orients you toward the outer world, and from the projections and introjections that create a sense of self. We speak of being *in* a body, as though the self were somehow contained inside a bodily exterior. Conversely, we understand the body as materiality held within an encompassing self-consciousness. The margin of your body is also a "social skin," an exterior meeting the social world that is also interior.[1] Inside and outside run imperceptibly into each other, as when you run your finger along the side of a Möbius strip.

Your body has and is a history. I continue to live in my body, which is, after all, the only one I'll ever have. When I'm teaching now, I gesture extravagantly as I always did, using my hands to shape my argument. I'm not thinking of these gestures, or conscious of the fact that my hands now are those of a quadriplegic, with fingers always bent into loose fists. I lack the strength to hold a pen. The outer part of each hand is innervated by nerves emerging from the spinal column a bit below my injury, which means that it's hard for me to move the small and ring fingers, which remain bent at the knuckle and can't really be flattened out. The thumb side of both right and left is stronger. Only with my thumbs can I feel the world pretty much, though not fully, as I used to, for the nerves governing them are the least damaged of all those running to my hands. When I am teaching, it's only as I drop my notes or fumble to turn a page that I am suddenly conscious of these embodied realities. Years and years of experiencing my hands as strong and capable laid down certain tracks in my mind and body. So I gesture without thinking when I speak, living as a body that no longer works or looks the way it did before the accident.

This is but one of a multitude of embodied realities that are simultaneously fantasies dwelling in my unconscious life. Proprioception, the sense of your body in space that you unconsciously experience all day long, is the medical term for a felt sense of the body that emerges over years of embodied life. You are from birth in deeply intimate relation to all the others who handle you and talk to you, and through their ministrations you begin to distinguish the zones of your body and differentiate among them. Through uncounted repetitions you learn to name your body parts, both feeling and knowing which piggy is going to market, and which cries wee, wee, wee all the way home. Once you learn to ride a bicycle, you don't have to think about it, you compose your body in relation to the machine and use "muscle memory" to keep your balance. Athletes spend countless hours repeating drills, training their muscles to respond without thinking according to the disciplines specific to their sport. But no one can move through the world without accurate proprioception. Feeling your organs inside, keeping your balance, reaching out to pick something up, sensing the distance to the seat of a chair—it's all proprioception.

Early on, Dr. Seetherama, my physiatrist, took hold of my big toe, told me not to look, and instructed me to tell him whether he was bending it up or down. So I did. I reported exactly what I felt. The problem was, I was wrong much of the time. It seemed odd to me then, and continues to seem so today that I could be misinformed by a part of my body I'd taken for granted always. My big toe! How could it be telling me the wrong information? Dr. Seetherama was testing my proprioception, and I failed the test. Now and then I ask Janet to repeat the test, and I fail every time. If the "felt sense" of my body is unreliable, how am I to think about the "bodily ego" that psychoanalysis theorizes is necessary to all of us, an image of the body that emerges internally through the differentiation of bodily parts and zones, and externally through relations with others?[2] What becomes of my "self"?

7

✳

Masculine, Feminine,
or Fourth of July

Babe the Dog was a lab and golden retriever mix, born on the Fourth of July, or at least close enough that I could claim the parades and fireworks as a celebration of that auspicious event. At home the dog would get an extra Milk-Bone treat, and the people would get a mint chocolate chip ice cream cake with chocolate fudge icing from Baskin-Robbins. When the local Baskin-Robbins closed, it was replaced by another ice cream franchise. What could we do? Janet called to place the order.

"We don't have fudge icing."

"What do you have?"

"Masculine, feminine, or Fourth of July."

"What? But . . . ," Janet stumbled, "but, we want *fudge*. And, and . . . it's for the *dog*—we have a dog, and it's her birthday."

Janet pressed the point but ended up just saying, "Whatever." I don't remember the icing, other than that it was disappointingly *not* fudge. Nor can I recall ordering again from that particular shop. I have, however, many times used the line "masculine, feminine, or Fourth of July" to teach both the absurdity and the normative power of gender. There in a list of choices are its two wholly naturalized categories and a comically out-of-place national holiday, but the seemingly misplaced Fourth of July serves to remind us that a laughably simple and punishingly binary notion of gender is enforced by the powers that be, including the state. Gender, which is a state of mind and embodied attitude, is a site of volatile power, pleasure, and subtle coercion, often used to discipline our thoughts and bodily affects. Normative gender is certainly wielded as a weapon by children anxious to shore up their own selfhood by challenging someone else's. Consult your memory and you'll find that this is true.

Sadly, madly, every birth certificate offers two—and only two—sexes, and only one may be declared. Sex is the first question in every mouth after a birth, and infants are quite ruthlessly assigned to one body or the other, despite the fact that intersex births are far more common than you would think, as the important work of biologist Ann Fausto-Sterling has demonstrated.[1] If innate biology offers no firm foundation for a superstructure of twos, neither does the social world. Parents, teachers, siblings, peers, physicians, pastors, psychologists, and those who enforce the law, all solicit a child to shelter itself under one gender or the other, but many kids refuse, sometimes at considerable cost to themselves.

Gender can also afford embodied pleasures, if one is confident in instantiating it and pleased with the results. It's now possible to modify your body to conform to your felt sense of gender. I've taught students who came to Wesleyan sexed and gendered as (more or less) feminine women, but graduated as trans men (FTM) with deepened voices and beards, their bodies modified by top surgeries—the removal of breasts—and shots of testosterone (T). There's no necessity dictating that a bodymind sexed female at birth will present itself to the world as feminine in adulthood, and no necessary sexuality tied to either sex or gender. "[T]he longer I hang around the various crossroads and deltas of gender, the more I notice that nothing is clear enough to be easy," writes S. Bear Bergman, a trans man who's hung around long enough to be well recognized in the queer-trans community as an author of first-person accounts.[2] Today young people who transform their official gender may be accepted, even celebrated—more than one transgender girl has been elected homecoming queen—but transgender teenagers have been murdered in school, too. Larry (Latisha) King, a slight, effeminate fifteen-year-old boy relentlessly hounded as a "faggot," was killed, shot in the head by a high school classmate offended by Latisha's feminine bearing, flirtatious manner, makeup, and high-heeled boots.[3] Children yoked with a gender they don't recognize as their own or who are confused can be made to suffer cruelly in a world that naturalizes and links together binary sex and gender. If you make it into young adulthood, you may be able to use the force field of gender for your own pleasure and toward your own ends, but straight is the gate and narrow the way.

Once I got to college, I didn't give much thought to my gender and devoted lots to my sexuality. Most of the time I wore flannel shirts and jeans, sneakers and boots. The first lesbian activists in the gay liberation movement whom I met in 1972 declared themselves relieved that they now could go to the bars liberated from the felt necessity to identify as either butch or femme. So those gendered sexualities seemed to me and my friends a thing of the past, something to be playfully gestured toward but not seriously taken up. In the spring of my senior year, for instance, I picked up a black tuxedo jacket at a yard sale and stepped out to a big party wearing it with my freshly washed white painter pants. I stopped on the way to pick a white rose from the president's rose garden for my buttonhole, and joined my friends feeling quite dashing.

This sort of "soft butch" style was not, however, to be taken seriously, because we were lesbian feminists who thought that asserting masculine/feminine anywhere, by anyone, was a patriarchal dead end. Butch/femme was something to sport with rather than a deeply felt commitment to honor. Lesbian sexuality seemed to me to have nothing to do with masculinity—or femininity, for that matter, though lesbianism was integral to a feminism that sought to liberate all women. Sex was just sexy. Commitments to explicitly feminine and masculine styles were to my mind outmoded and irrelevant. I've done a lot of reading and talking since then, and have come to regret this position so insensitive to the complexities of desire and the stylizations specific to race and class, but such was my youthful understanding. When several years ago I read Amber Hollibaugh's book *My Dangerous Desires*, I recognized myself as one who would have discounted her and her sweetheart had we met in the 1970s. She's a big, beautiful, dedicated femme who showed up with her decidedly butch lover at a meeting where they were both written off as relics of a superseded past. She was rejected by a movement for sexual liberation she'd been a part of from the first. Amber, please accept my apologies.

* * *

In the 1950s and 1960s, one place butch/femme genders were elaborated was working-class bar culture—you can get a vivid sense of the stakes by reading *Stone Butch Blues*, an autobiographical bildungsroman that recounts how a young butch comes of age in the bars and factories of Buffalo, New York. For another approach to the same scene, read *Boots of Leather, Slippers of Gold*, an oral history of working-class lesbian life that famously dedicates itself to "understand[ing] butch-fem culture from an insider's perspective." (Both books have been recently reissued, clear evidence of ongoing interest in how gender is stylized.)[4] My lover in graduate school was older than I, and had grown up in a lower-middle-class neighborhood surrounded by New Jersey affluence. She wanted to have nothing to do with the culture of those bars. When I was in graduate school, Elizabeth and I once went to a bar in Pawtucket, a worn-out working-class town just north of Providence. The place was mostly empty, though several women were playing pool, most of them large, all with short haircuts, wearing shirts and pants. It seemed sad and lifeless to Elizabeth, though I could imagine having fun drinking Miller High Life and hanging out in a place so far distant from my library carrel. I drank a Miller and she had a bad glass of wine. We never returned.

Elizabeth's dislike was, I think, solidly grounded in a refusal to be identified with a lower-class stylization of life. Her mother, a gifted seamstress, conspired with her daughter to transform Elizabeth into a girl who could, without any faltering and with no misstep, date a boy who belonged to the Windy Hollow Hunt Club and rode to hounds. He invited her to the annual Hunt Ball, and had the pleasure of a beautiful, fashionable date on his arm. Elizabeth said he was handsome, but dumb as a brick. Things started looking up her first year in college, when she fell in love with a Jewish girl from New York City—a striver like herself, but from a world entirely different from suburban New Jersey. I don't know what her girlfriend studied, but Elizabeth was a French major who longed for the elegance and intellectual sophistication of Paris. When they graduated in 1962, they were off to the City of Lights.

Elizabeth was to return to Paris again and again, first as a graduate student studying the most experimental of experimental French novels, and then as a professor of French language and literature. When she spoke to me of those years, she told me that the Katmandou, a nightclub at 21 rue Vieux Colombier, was fabulous, and when we went together to Paris in 1990, we hoped to find it still open, only to be disappointed. I discovered an Internet site memorializing its history when I googled the name.[5] It was "a sophisticated place, patronized by relatively well-heeled women and celebrities, whether lesbian or not: the place was therefore quite exclusive socially," and promised attractive decadence. As the club's publicity pointedly announced, "The girls are young, modern, [and wear] miniskirts, [not the] antique male costume of the other clubs."

* * *

When Janet and I took up gender in the waning years of the 1990s, I once again sported with "masculinity," while Janet elaborated a fabulous "femininity" for her amusement and mine. In those years, lesbian genders often reprised butch and femme styles in a purportedly "postmodern" sort of way—it was the era of the *Rocky Horror Picture Show* revival on Broadway and doing the time warp dance ("Oh, fantasy free me . . .").[6] We dressed for our own pleasure, certainly, but also as a way of being quickly legible as lesbians. Butches have it easier, in that regard, than femme lesbians, who are almost always read as heterosexual—except when in a butch-femme couple. When we would "go to New York," as we called it when going to some cultural event in the city, we'd dress up, as we did once when heading out for a decidedly feminist/queer musical put on by the rock 'n' roll band Betty. I vividly remember leaving the apartment, because the lobby had a huge mirror that reflected our happiness and high style—I was in a white silk shirt with French cuffs, gold and silver cufflinks (Janet's gift, from Tiffany's no less!), black velvet jacket, red leather boot-cut pants, and black cowboy boots. Janet wore a long-sleeved white shirt that you could see right through, a sleeveless shirt with an icon of the Virgin Mary on its front, a short gray skirt, and gorgeous red pumps with four-inch heels. Off to the first show, we were walking together in the evening light, and on the busy sidewalk passed a homeless man. We dropped our loose change in his cup, and as we walked away he called loudly after us, "You're *both* lesbians!" That short sentence quickly became shorthand for the pleasures of dressing up and stepping out.

In colder weather, instead of the velvet jacket I wore a butter-soft, mid-calf black leather coat with a white silk scarf. The coat had a beautiful satin lining that afforded scant protection in the wintertime, a fact that was borne in on me one January night when we were walking from the subway to a bar called Hell, in the meatpacking district where the wind whips off the Hudson River—but who cares? Janet had a delectable array of bustiers, filmy blouses, leather, velvet, and silk skirts, and many heels, including brown knee-high boots with silver tips from Barney's and those red pumps—so elegant that they were long on display in our bedroom. In 2003 we went to Provincetown over Memorial Day weekend to celebrate Janet's birthday. We were dressed up and on our way to a restaurant for a celebratory meal when a guy sitting on a porch set back from the street hollered out, "You sexy things!" Who's to argue? We both loved making it clear that we were sexual partners, and that we were, as the phrase is, "sex-positive" and queer.

The last time I can remember dressing up this way was to go to a cocktail party Henry was throwing early in the fall semester of 2003, maybe three weeks before I broke my neck. Janet and I were apart, in Middletown and NYC. Because wearing black leather jeans requires a certain frame of mind, in the absence of Janet I was seriously considering how I wanted to dress up for the party. In the end, I decided that such an event hosted by one of the founders of the field of queer studies actually called for those leather jeans, which I chose to complement with a tight, silky, white sleeveless top that did a great job of showing off not only my breasts, but also biceps, triceps, deltoids, and pecs. Silver earrings, silver bracelet, silver rings. Fendi perfume. I got to flirt with the girls *and* the boys—it was a great outfit and just the right gender for the occasion.

* * *

I no longer have a gender. Rather, I have a wheelchair. I'm entirely absorbed into its gestalt. I'm now misrecognized as a man more often than ever before, almost every time I go out. I'm not surprised. I know that 82% of spinal cord injuries are suffered by young men, and middle-aged butchy women must be statistically negligible in that accounting. Besides, when I'm outside wheeling my chair, I'm belted in. For ten years, I used a three-inch belt that went around my chest and fastened with Velcro—I grabbed each end, pushed my torso against the seat back, and brought the belt together as high up on my chest and as tightly as I could, but it still did a pretty good job of flattening my breasts. This I regarded as a great irony and a perverse injury, because I've never wanted to bind my breasts, unlike some butch women. To the contrary, I used to wear my shirts unbuttoned at the top, as Janet likes to remind me, and my zippers pulled down almost to the cleavage. I like my big, gorgeous breasts. I now have a higher back to my wheelchair and a neoprene vest to hold me up, with straps coming down over my shoulders to keep them back, and straps at the bottom, just under my rib cage, that are secured to the side of the chair. There's a zipper up the middle. My breasts are not as smashed by this restraint, which I wear all the time. It's better for my posture, if not for my wardrobe. I joke with Janet that the vest reminds me of the old advertisements for Maidenform bras that "lift and separate." There's no "lifting" in this case, only a unisex sort of flattening, and indifferent separating. I love my breasts, and loved to show them off, but there's no way you'd know that seeing me now.

It's actually impossible for me to sit up straight, though it took me two years to understand that simple fact. My body is flat enough when I lie down, but when I sit up, my spine is shaped like a C. Not one of my "core" muscles is functional—those muscles that you work so hard in Pilates—the ones around your abdomen and back that support your torso. "Rake the seat of the chair from front to back," Danielle, my life-affirming physical therapist, said to me. We were talking about the wheelchair I was using in the Hospital for Special Care. "Look, it's built so that you can make the adjustment, using the holes that are drilled right here. You can raise the front so it dumps you on your tailbone. Let gravity work for you." I did as she instructed when I got my own chair, so when I'm seated, I'm always slightly reclined. Check out your own body, and imagine that the muscles below the breastbone have little functional power—you'd flop over without support, like I do. To make things worse, the C-curve of my back is accentuated because the surgery on my neck thrusts my head slightly forward, like a pigeon's when it walks. As I sit slumped in the chair, the chair is what you see. That's my distinctive profile.

I may have no gender, but the chair does. It's masculine. True, most of the time I offer little that would help you see me as a woman. I dress all in black—black pants or dark jeans, black T-shirt, black sweater. The chair is black, the vest is black, and I'm trying to make my body disappear as much as I can. When I am dressing for work, I'll wear a colorful scarf and earrings, but that's it. Maybe I am in permanent mourning. When somebody refers to me as a man, or calls me sir, and then realizes the mistake, profuse apologies follow, as if I had just suffered a grievous insult. The man stocking the grocery store shelves the other day, the shopper in front of me, the boy in the elevator, the barista at the coffee shop, the poll worker where I went to vote—I say to them all, "That's okay. It doesn't matter." The woman standing chatting on the sidewalk tells her friend, "Let that man pass." Then, flustered, "Oh, I'm so sorry. I just didn't realize, I didn't see, I couldn't tell . . ." "Don't worry—it's okay," I say, as I pass by.

And it is. I just don't care that much about my gender, which perhaps tells you all you need to know about how alien I find my body, how alien my life can feel to me.

8

✳

Time Held Me
Green and Dying

I learned to ride a bicycle when I was living with my parents and my brother in the Mission House, where I spent the first six years of my life. It's a two-story brick building with four apartments that kept its name when it was used as faculty housing, rather than as shelter for missionaries on furlough from the mission field. It keeps the name still, although it currently endures the rough usage of students. Juniata College was founded by the Church of the Brethren, and continues to be part of that tradition, though I'm sure there are both students and faculty working there now who know little of its history as an institution of the church. My father was a professor of history, as my mother had been a professor of home economics before the birth of my brother. I remember some pretty impressive bicycle accidents from those days—I rode off the short retaining wall by the side of the Mission House, for instance, and crashed onto the sidewalk below. Then there was the accident when I lost control riding "no hands" down the hill from Taylor Highlands towards the intersection with Moore Street below. Skidding on the pavement gave me impressively bloody brush burns, the injury cyclists call "road rash." An adult appeared. He asked me where I lived, gathered me into the front of his pickup, and put my bicycle in the back. I think of Spartans carried home on their shields. When I was sixteen, my parents bought me a ten-speed, a glossy green Schwinn Varsity. Built with a steel frame, it was a tank. I rode it, nonetheless, around the hilly countryside of central Pennsylvania. One summer day, I was on the Petersburg Pike, coming down fast where the road drops steeply toward the intersection with Route 26, when a bee flew into my blue work shirt and stung me right on my *nipple*. It says something about my mature bicycle handling skills that I somehow managed to stop at the stop sign, and pedal safely home. I could tell you in considerable detail about every bicycle I've had since then, and other accidents averted, but the bike that matters now is the second Schwinn in my life, that light, bright machine I bought for myself when forty years old.

Because I'd always used my bike as a way to get from one place to another, I was accustomed to riding with books or bags of groceries lashed to the back rack. I'm pretty sure that I wouldn't have seriously taken up cycling as a sport had I not known John. I got to know him because he was Elizabeth's best friend—they went through graduate school together, and for a while they were lovers. Elizabeth lived in Providence, he in a small town outside of New London. They visited each other regularly, and talked on the phone nearly every day. As Elizabeth and I spent time together, we together saw John, and often would go to his home in semirural Connecticut to play together of an afternoon, and stay for dinner in the evening. Sometimes we would just stroll out to his garden to admire the green beans and the sunflowers and the profusion of pumpkins that had shown up as volunteers in his compost pile. More often, the three of us would ride the slow back roads of Connecticut, ten, twenty, forty miles looping out from his house and back. No matter which route you took, the first part would be downhill, more or less steeply, depending on the direction you set out. I, of course, loved the steep slopes. I would get down "in the drops" (my hands on the lowest part of the handlebars, underneath the curve) and pedal hard. Before long I would spin out of my largest gear, tuck into my most aerodynamic position, and watch the road rush by, while keeping an eye on my speedometer— once I hit forty miles an hour, and I was always hoping to go faster, faster. John, whose bike was geared higher, would always be out in front, and I would always be chasing him.

He had been riding since his college days in the early sixties. I have a newspaper clipping his mother, Mary, gave to me, that shows him competing in the annual Little 500, a bicycle race held by fraternities to raise money for Indiana University's scholarship fund. A lovely little movie, *Breaking Away* (1979), which won both a Golden Globe and an Oscar, accorded the event brief national fame and, along with Greg LeMond's Tour de France victories, brought bicycle racing significant publicity in America. In the 1980s it was, nonetheless, still unusual to see a grown man riding a bicycle with a custom-made frame, skinny tires, clip-in pedals, and a tiny pack holding a repair kit for a punctured tire underneath the narrow leather racing saddle. He was, furthermore, dressed in black Lycra cycling shorts and a bright red cycling jersey with a banana (quick-peel energy food) stuck in the back pocket. Because John wore cycling shoes with cleats that snapped into his pedals (rather than the outdated toe clips that were on the bikes Elizabeth and I rode), he had to walk his bike down the winding dirt drive to the road, and sit down there to put on his shoes, leaving his sandals stashed in the mailbox. We ribbed him about that little ceremony, and, because he was a modest man, Elizabeth would tease him for venturing out in those skin-tight shorts. Before too long, however, when we went out for rides, all three of us wore skin-tight shorts padded in the seat, because they really are more comfortable when you're on a bike. It took me a lot longer to upgrade to a high-quality, light, properly fitted road bicycle and buy the necessary snap-in cycling shoes. John kept at me, saying it'll be great, you'll see, and he went with me to his shop, where he knew the guys, to help me pick out the only brand-new bike I ever bought for myself.

John was quite handsome and just over six feet tall, a kind, generous, and energetic man who laughed a lot. He was really strong. I loved him as a brother, kidded around with him and competed with him, knowing full well I would lose every time. I learned from him that when you are riding a bicycle, you are always either chasing or breaking away—in short, either trying to close the gap between yourself and a rider ahead, or charging out in front of those around you so as to create an unbridgeable distance in the imaginary race you are riding with imaginary competitors. (Remember playing sandlot baseball with imaginary runners on base?) In the years that Elizabeth and I were riding with John, there wasn't much press or TV coverage of cycling—hardly any at all—and certainly no mainstream discussion of the tactics and strategies of bicycle racing. He subscribed to the magazine *Bicycling*, which I would leaf through, but the little I knew about proper cycling position on the bike John taught me, and everything I knew about racing came from him.

Riding in a paceline, for example. Bicycle races feature teams of cyclists who, for much of the race, are grouped together in what's called the peloton, which offers a considerable reduction in effort (up to 40%) to those riding in the slipstream of the cyclists who are out in front breaking the wind.[1] Different teams will strategically move to the front of the peloton at different times, depending on the standing of the strongest rider on the team, which means that the whole large group is going faster than any individual possibly could ride. Any small number of cyclists who manage to break away from that pack must cooperate with one another by forming a paceline, or the peloton, with its numerical and aerodynamic advantage, will certainly chase them down. One day John and I went out together.

We were down out of the hills and on the approach to Mystic that is relatively flat, three to four miles along the Mystic River as it flows toward the harbor and beyond. "Let's see how fast we can go," John proposed excitedly. "Just get right on my rear wheel and follow as closely as you can—after a couple of minutes, when I'm tired, I'll move to the left and drift back and you'll take the front position." So I rode with my head down and hands over the hoods of the brakes so as to keep my body low, and tried to stay as close to his wheel as I could manage without clipping it and throwing him off balance. When he moved to the side and tucked in behind me, I was suddenly out in front, breaking the wind. It was so much harder! Protected by John, I hadn't registered the fact that a stiff headwind was blowing in from Long Island Sound. I kept my cadence high and tried not to drop too far off the pace he had set, but before long I had to motion him forward and drift back behind. Then I discovered just how much stronger a cyclist he really was. I tried my best to stay right on his rear wheel, keeping my torso low, but I was forced to shift down into a lower gear to keep my cadence steady, and soon I was feet, not inches, from John's wheel, and then yards, and then many yards . . . "Hey, John," I hollered, "wait up, wait up! Wait up!!" That's when I learned that the rider behind exerts 75–80% to the leader's 100%. I had exhausted myself on my first "pull," and John simply rode away from me when out in front again.

After we went through Mystic and were back inland, John proposed that we try again. "Let's go flat out from here to the turnoff—it's about five miles, no real hills." "Um, uh, okay." Off we went. With no headwind, I was better able to contribute to our joint effort, coming to the fore when John would move to the side, though he was able to sustain the lead position longer than I. I gave maximum effort, surging *over* rises in the road, body *forward*, standing *up* on the pedals for better leverage, pushing *through* the rotation at the bottom of the circle—simply willing myself *not* to shift down into an easier gear, and *not* to drop off the cadence—all the while struggling to do the very simplest arithmetic in my oxygen-deprived head . . . how many minutes will it take, dear God, to go 5 miles at 20 miles an hour, uh, 21, 23 . . . how many minutes have passed? Could time possibly be slowing d.o.w.n and d . . o . . . w . . . . n and d . . . o . . . . w . . . . . n . . . . ? How . . . Much . . . . Longer . . . . . . Then SUDDENLY John sat up, flung his hands in the air, and turned around toward me as he began to coast. "Wasn't that FUN? WASN'T THAT GREAT?" And it was, it was really great to be playing like that with a boy, completely absorbed in the physical challenge—I loved it. I loved him.

The only bicycle race I've ever ridden in was with John. It was an official amateur event held in New London, a mile-long course laid out on the city streets for a "criterium," ten times around the same one-mile loop. It happened before the Silver Streak, when I was still riding a bicycle I'd bought secondhand while in graduate school, while John rode his fancy European bike. My bike had a scratched-up orange frame, regular (fat) bike tires, a rack for carrying stuff mounted in the back, a bag under the seat with the kit to fix flats and an extra inner tube, reflectors everywhere—mine looked like the working road bike it was, not a racing machine. I took off the rack and the bag, but there wasn't much else I could do, and I looked kind of silly lined up there with all the other competitors. My great victory was a negative one. I was *not* lapped by other cyclists, and thereby ushered out of the race altogether. John finished far ahead of me, after dropping me on the first turn. Not only was his bicycle "light as a feather," as Elizabeth was fond of pointing out, but he was a much, much stronger cyclist. I knew that however much I upgraded my equipment I'd never be his equal.

* * *

In early June 1995, Elizabeth and I rode together with John in a fund-raising event for the Multiple Sclerosis Society, riding in support of Jeff, who was then serving as the chair of the Lancaster, Pennsylvania, chapter of the Society. I got T-shirts made for the three of us, white, with TEAM CROSBY written above a great color photo of Jeff, Beth, and the kids. The ride was seventy-five miles out to a college campus where we were put up overnight, and seventy-five miles back the next day. On the second day, as riders gathered to start, there was a problem with a friend's bicycle, so we waved John off, knowing he wanted to ride hard. And so he did, joining with a couple guys in a paceline that was one of the first groups over the finish line, hours before Elizabeth and I arrived. I regard that fact as astonishing, because his abdomen was full of metastatic melanoma tumors.

In his early thirties, Elizabeth had seen him through a surgery that carved a malignant melanoma tumor out of his back, and a large margin around it, besides, before grafting skin from his thigh to cover the wound. He wasn't supposed to survive the first five years, but he did, then six, seven, and after ten years symptom-free he was no longer on high alert waiting for it to come back. He didn't forget about it though, and seventeen years after the surgery, when he felt enlarged lymph nodes in his left armpit, he was scared. Surgery to remove the affected nodes was "successful," but lymph circulates throughout the body, and metastatic melanoma is a killer untouched by chemo, as he and Elizabeth understood all too well. Five years later, in August, he thought he felt an abdominal tumor, tried to talk himself out of it, felt it again, and yet again, had surgery, and started an experimental treatment using interferon/interleukin to boost his immune system, which required hospitalization every third week and made him violently ill. His oncologist opened him up again on February 14, hoping to cut out any malignancies not destroyed by the treatment, but instead discovered incipient tumors in their earliest manifestation spread all through his abdominal cavity. Elizabeth wept at the bitter irony of this fatal Valentine. John returned to the treatment. She looked for any possible advantage, willing him to survive—an organic herbal tea, a fish oil. He told her that sometimes lying awake at night without moving, he felt okay, and imagined going downstairs to make a peanut butter sandwich as he used to do. How he missed that life! As much as she longed not to lose him, he longed to live.

When we three did the MS ride at the beginning of June, he was still strong. Not for long. He continued the course of interferon/interleukin—it was his only chance, however unlikely to succeed, and giving it up was unthinkable, tantamount to admitting defeat. In late July, his physician slipped a Medi-Port under the skin of his chest, with a catheter connected directly to a vein and a port through which medicine could drip or be injected, to save John the punctures of repeated IVs. A buildup of fluid in his abdomen was becoming intolerable, so a physician inserted a needle into his peritoneal cavity to drain it. In August, his mother, Mary, came from Indiana to care for him, once again bringing food to his lips and arranging his pillows, tending him as she had done at the beginning of his life. Elizabeth and I did what we could. When the two of us, one on each side, helped him to the bathroom for what turned out to be the last shower he'd ever take, I saw how truly weak and emaciated his body had become, as the tumors grew and grew, monopolizing his metabolism. His abdomen continued to swell. We were with him down to the hopeless, helpless days of waiting for death by his bed, as the last urine his body would produce slowly dripped dark amber into a

Foley bag. He was a strong man who wanted to live, and dying was hard work. By mid-September it was over.

When I reflect on it, I'm once again astonished that he successfully completed the 150-mile MS fundraiser, riding so strongly the second day, because we all knew perfectly well that he was sick. You could already see that his abdomen was slightly distended. Sometime toward the end I learned the word "ascites," the technical name for fluid that leaks into the abdomen when the liver is seriously compromised. As it happened, all of his organs were destined for failure, although none of us could admit of such a possibility in early June. (It's only late in the process that you understand the arrival of dying, I've found.) Snapshots we took at a rest stop show the swelling. You can see the slight curve under the Lycra of his cycling shorts—there we are, nonetheless, happily eating oranges, and there's John, looking so good, squinting against the sun and laughing. As we set off again, he discovered a broken spoke in his front wheel, so he and I stayed behind while a helpful volunteer mechanic replaced it. As we rode off together, he called out, "Let's go!" We hammered down and overtook the others before they reached the next rest stop, much to their astonishment. He wanted no truck with death.

When my new bicycle arrived in early July, I thought first of riding with John, so Elizabeth and I planned with him to leave from his house and ride down through Mystic and back. We started off coasting downhill and then took the quiet, beautiful back road along the Mystic River, but when we got into town, he asked to stop. We sat down at a sidewalk café. He was white and exhausted. There was no way he was getting back on his bike. He called a friend, who showed up with an SUV, and that truncated ride was my last with John.

* * *

There's a term I learned watching the Tour de France on TV—*hors catégorie*, or "beyond class." It's reserved for roads over the Alps and Pyrenees that are so difficult as to exceed the classification system used to categorize a climb by factors that include its length and degree of incline. Difficult beyond belief, difficult beyond measure.

John asked that Dylan Thomas's poem "Fern Hill" be read at his memorial service. The speaker of the poem begins by imagining a "green and golden time" when "I was young and easy under the apple boughs," and allows those years to emerge in gorgeous, glorious detail. Alas, the poem turns from life to death in the lush fatality of this concluding stanza.

> Nothing I cared, in the lamb white days, that time would take me
> Up to the swallow thronged loft by the shadow of my hand,
> In the moon that is always rising,
> Nor that riding to sleep
> I should hear him fly with the high fields
> And wake to the farm forever fled from the childless land.
> Oh as I was young and easy in the mercy of his means,
> Time held me green and dying
> Though I sang in my chains like the sea.[2]

John spent many summer days of his childhood with his grandfather on the farm in Indiana where his mother grew up, and had a framed aerial picture of its acres hanging next to his fireplace. Rolling, startlingly green fields surround the barn and farmhouse with its stand of trees, but neither he nor his brother wanted to work the land, so it passed from the family. John fought against death every way he knew how, but to no avail.

Can sorrow be measured on the pain scale running from 0—no grief—to 10—the worst grief you can imagine? No. Neither pain nor sorrow will suffer to be quantified, but remain beyond compare. *Hors catégorie.*

9

✱

Jefferson Clark Crosby

On January 5, 2010, my brother, Jeff, died. He was fifty-seven and almost completely paralyzed from multiple sclerosis—he could move his head side to side, but not raise it up off his pillow, and his limbs, hands, and torso had long since failed him. Perhaps he got a urinary tract infection that was too much for his diminished body to fight off, or maybe it was something else. No matter. Over the course of five days his lungs began to fill with fluid as his heart could no longer pump strongly enough to circulate oxygenated blood. For five days, his breathing grew more and more labored, with mucus rattling in every breath, until his struggle was over.

When I first learned from our parents that Jeff had been diagnosed with MS, I was twenty-seven and he was twenty-eight. Beth had a few months earlier delivered their first child, Kirsten. Actually, what Mother and Dad told me in their first phone call was that he was in the hospital undergoing tests to figure out why he couldn't control his legs properly, a fact that was increasingly evident when he tried to move laterally on the racquetball court. He was accustomed to excelling athletically, and he relished competition. He was strong, well-balanced, with terrific hand-eye coordination. But now something was wrong. The tests went on and on, one possibility after another coming up negative. Then my parents called again to say that he was being discharged, having been diagnosed with a progressive autoimmune disease that has no cure. His immune system had begun to launch attacks on the myelin that sheathes a neural cell's axon, down which ions pass. Myelin contains the electrical charge as insulation sheaths an electric cord. Inflammation and scarring result in sclerosis, a pathological hardening of tissue that destroys its function. Without healthy myelin, neural systems cannot function properly.

I bought a book, of course. This was in the early eighties, long before Google changed how you get information, and I knew nothing about the disease. About halfway through I stopped reading. The tone of the book was upbeat, relentlessly cheerful in the face of a recent diagnosis, belying the miseries that could await the sufferer: blindness, mental confusion, loss of coordination and strength, paralysis, pressure wounds, sexual dysfunction, urinary incontinence, bowel dysfunction, spasticity, and an early death, probably from organ failure, probably in one's fifties. It was frightening as hell. Each individual sufferer's course of the disease is different, and there was no way of knowing how Jeff's would play out. Some experience an intermittent MS, whereby an attack will be followed by recovery as the nervous system compensates for what has been lost by rerouting a network, only to be followed again by another attack. With every exacerbation, function is lost and never fully restored, so the trajectory over time is inevitably, but slowly, downward. Some, on the other hand, decline rapidly and die in a few years. Some decline more slowly, but steadily, without remission. No one experiences all the horrible symptoms. Jeff never went blind, did not suffer from neurological pain, nor was he confused. To the contrary, for many years, when talking with him on the telephone, it was easy to believe that nothing was wrong. The disease in him, however, was unremitting, and with each passing day he became more ill. Even in my late twenties, I knew that "the fifties" would be upon us all too soon.

* * *

When he was diagnosed, he had just completed law school and was working a prestigious job as a law clerk to a federal judge in Detroit. Jeff and Beth started living with MS just as his daughter, Kirsten, was born and his clerkship ended. In snapshots from that time, he stands close to Beth, or cradles Kirsten, showing no outward signs of being ill. But he would stumble, or have difficulty rising from a crouch. He and Beth had before them a choice. He could join a well-established labor law firm in Detroit, at which he had clerked when still a law student, and whose partners drove Cadillacs and worked all the time, or he could take a job with a small firm—only three partners—doing a general practice in the small Pennsylvania city of Lancaster. Both firms knew he had MS. The Pennsylvania job would put him in the bosom of our extended family on our mother's side, the aunts, uncles, and cousins with whom we celebrated every holiday, almost all of whom live close to Lancaster.

They chose the Lancaster firm, and moved to Lititz, the small town where Mother had grown up, about ten miles outside of the city. They decided, moreover, to buy from our uncle a white brick house that Jeff and I knew intimately. Built by our grandfather, 40 South Broad Street had been Mother's childhood home. The property has a stable out back that once had housed Papa's black horse, Prince, and when we were kids it still smelled just a little like a stable, even though long since it had been made into a garage. There was a big backyard with sour cherry trees that had supplied the filling for many pies when we were growing up. Jeff and Beth packed everything into a big U-Haul truck and two VW vans, theirs and Mother and Dad's. I had come along to help with the move, and the whole family drove our little caravan across the country to Lititz. Their decision to leave Detroit, to work for Gibbel, Kraybill, and Hess, to buy the house in which Mother grew up, and to join the Lititz Church of the Brethren where generations of our family had worshiped, was influenced by the fact of MS and the uncertain future he faced. Better to be among family, in a familiar place, working in a small firm with partners who valued fatherhood, family, service to others, and a simpler way of living. No Cadillacs. A Brethren way of life.

For years he worked 8:00–6:00 Monday through Friday and a half day on Saturday. Beth and he had another child, a boy they named Colin. Beth had an MAT in teaching and worked part-time as a tutor for students from Linden Hall, a private school for girls in Lititz. She was the homemaker, who shopped, cooked, cleaned, and took care of the children. She even ironed Jeff's shirts in the beginning. It was clear to me then, as it is now, that Beth's labor made it possible for Jeff to work as he did. I think those years, when his kids were young and he was still pretty able, came to have a golden glow for him as his abilities declined. How could they not? There he is in a photograph, in the glory of young fatherhood, tossing his son up into the air, as Colin screams with laughter. Or he is seated in the lemon-lime two-seater MGB convertible that he drove around the quiet back roads of Lancaster County, with the towheaded kids belted in behind—he made a place for them to sit that had been originally intended for luggage. The grazing cows slowly look up and the still air smells of manure and hay.

When they first moved to Lititz, he was strong and capable. In a snapshot of the U-Haul out in the alley behind the old stable, Jeff's in a T-shirt and shorts, wearing laced-up Red Wing work boots, standing on the bed of the truck and poised to jump down. He's so handsome with his brown beard, strikingly blue eyes, and muscular build. He looks so strong, as he indeed was. Yet even in that moment he had MS. Then he couldn't operate the clutch of the MGB anymore, and had to sell it. He started using a cane. He and Beth began looking for a new house when the walk from the back, where he parked in Prince's stall, proved to be too long. They moved from Lititz to a one-level house in an older suburb of Lancaster. Then he needed a folding wheelchair to use when standing was too hard and walking difficult—or sometimes even impossible. He began to use the chair all the time, and one day he was no longer able to make the transfer from it to the driver's seat of their red VW van. He bought another van, also red, though disappointingly not a VW—a full-size Chevy, modified to meet his needs. He steered by grasping a knob on the steering wheel, and controlled the throttle and the brakes with a lever on the left-hand side of the steering column. The van was fitted with a wheelchair lift, because he was in his chair full-time. A lockbox (6″ x 10″ x 2½″) was installed on the floor in the empty space where the driver's seat had been, and he would maneuver his chair until a bolt underneath would be caught by clamps in the box, and click-lock him in place.

* * *

Through all these changes he continued to look much like "himself." He sat upright in his chair, wore a suit and tie when dressed for work, and easily, even triumphantly showed off his skills, bumping down steps, popping up over curbs. Some years later, my cousin Barb, who works in Lancaster General Hospital as a social worker, made a passing remark that he was starting to look different, so I intentionally tried to see him anew. She was right. As he entered his forties, his abdominal muscles slowly started to fail, and he could no longer sit easily upright in his wheelchair. Looking at him I realized that his gestalt was newly nonnormative. The muscles of his back and abdomen were weakening, and his torso, once muscular above his bathing suit and brown in the summer sun, began to very slowly collapse down on itself, like a melting cone from Dairy Queen. And now he needed a battery-powered chair, which he would control with a joystick. The pace of the paralysis seemed to me to have quickened, but it may be simply that I saw him only two or three times a year, and his voice on the phone was unchanged. When we visited next, I noticed he had a Velcro belt coming under his armpits and over his chest, which had to be belted when he was out and about, and without which he could not drive, because he would simply pitch forward at the waist.

Janet and I went to see him when his marriage was failing, and he and Beth were separated. It was a couple of years before my accident. Beth stayed in the house with the kids, and he moved into one of the few accessible apartments for rent in Lancaster, a little basement studio with one window up high. Everything suddenly seemed changed for the worse. One of the times when he was assembling the help he would need to live alone, I was with him. He was on the phone, and was evidently asked what kind of assistance he required. "Well, for starters, I need help with dressing and undressing, and getting in and out of bed, and help with just about everything in the bathroom— shaving, brushing my teeth, getting on and off the toilet . . ." As he continued with the list, I suddenly understood his life differently. I simply hadn't known—or wanted to know—how dependent he had become, because I didn't see the work of producing him as the public person who rolled out of the master bedroom (with its newly constructed, en suite, fully accessible bathroom) that he shared with Beth, ready for work, looking like the lawyer he was. I wanted him to simply be that person. I hadn't fully realized that he could no longer do much of *anything* that required fine motor skills, and had lost the ability to independently transfer himself into or out of the chair.

Large and small muscles alike were giving way, as his neurological system developed ever more fatally hardened plaques. All the intimate, invisible work such a devastating physical decline entails was, I'm sure, a grave complication for a twenty-four-year marriage that was, of course, a complex history of intimacy. I have no wish to recount that relationship from my point of view. Whatever intolerable negative surplus brought them to divorce, the MS that shaped their adulthood objectively became a heavier and heavier burden—but a weight carried in the privacy of the bedroom and bathroom. The labor of moving him on and off the toilet, helping him first on, and then off of the shower bench, waiting while he used the joystick to maneuver the chair over into position by the sink, then squeezing toothpaste onto his toothbrush and waiting for him to brush his teeth, putting on the super-tight compression knee socks he wore against edema, rolling the external catheter onto his penis and then attaching it to his leg bag, and *finally* getting him dressed—these jobs were invisible to me until he was no longer living with Beth, and I started helping him.

When Janet and I came to visit, the aide who would come from an agency wouldn't come, and I would help him. "Look, Tina—here it is, rolled up. Just put it on like you do a condom." I looked at him. He looked at me. "That's a useless comparison for me, you silly boy," I said. And then we laughed and laughed. Helping with his body brought us closer together. I came to understand in great detail that Jeff's body had really changed, and would continue to change. He would need more and more help.

In an essay he wrote four years before he died, Jeff recounts how asking for help can be a gift to the one who offers assistance. There you are in your wheelchair, and people want to help, sometimes coming up without being asked. If he didn't need any help, Jeff would quietly and politely say he'd like to be as independent as possible. As he became less able, he realized that asking for assistance could be an opportunity for someone to enjoy the pleasure of giving. He asked for help openly, even of people he didn't know, or knew only slightly. Rather than conceptualizing his need for help as nothing but diminishment, he realized that many people wished to ease his way. He wrote a short essay, "I Believe in the Importance of Asking," that was aired on the local NPR radio station in their series of "This I Believe." In it he narrates how he became progressively and inexorably more dependent. When he wrote the piece, he was unable even to scratch his nose, because he could no longer lift his arms, and his hands were long since quite useless. Yet he concludes, "The power of asking is my only growing power these days. And it truly is a power that's most important. Asking has taught me that I'm not MS—it's only a part of me." His empathetic interest in the lives of others drew people to him, and his openness about his needs was most often attractive, not repellent. How he lived with his incapacities made him the man whom others wished to help and befriend, making the disease secondary, despite its destructive power.

When he wrote his essay, he was living in the nursing unit of the Moravian Manor, a continuing care community that our cousin Barb helped him get into when the time came for around-the-clock care. The community is run not by the Brethren, but by the Moravian Church, a Protestant denomination similarly harassed out of Germany in the seventeenth century. The property abuts that of the Lititz Church of the Brethren, and when Jeff lived in the Manor, he was able at first to ride his wheelchair over to church on Sunday morning. By the time he wrote on the importance of asking, he was spending more time in bed as it became harder and harder for him to summon the energy to sit up, and there was little incentive to transfer over into his chair, because he could no longer use the joystick to move it once he got there.

Throughout his life, Jeff fought for mobility, and didn't stop even though he was living in a nursing unit. He discovered on the Internet a new chair developed by a tech engineer living in California. The chair was controlled not by a joystick, but by pressure on a mouthpiece like a retainer—you would use your tongue to guide it left or right, forward or back. Jeff had been part of a Sunday school class for decades, and he told them about the chair, which cost $40,000. Led by his class, the congregation of the Lititz Church of the Brethren, with help from the church's district office, bought the chair for him. He preached a lay sermon not long after, and likened the gift to the miracle at the pool of Bethesda when Jesus bid a lame man to take up his bed and walk. The gift of the chair "manifests Christ's teaching through the action of our Brethren body," he told the congregation. The generosity of his brothers and sisters in Christ promised to ensure his continued mobility, and immeasurably relieved his mind. As it happened, repeated technical failures limited his use of the chair, and the discovery that the signal sent by the mouthpiece interfered with the wireless call system of the hospital strictly limited the hours he could use it anywhere outside his room. Yet even as it became little but an encumbrance in his small space, he remained deeply grateful for the generosity of his fellow congregants. He did not lose faith.

* * *

Jeff managed to get to the hospital when I was hurt, which happened right before he moved into the nursing unit of the Manor. I have a blurred half-memory of his wheelchair at the foot of the hospital bed. It was an enormous effort on his part, and I love him for it. Then, as I began to comprehend all I had lost, I was increasingly horrified at the apparent symmetry of my embodiment to Jeff's. I remembered the first time I heard him call himself "quadriplegic," a word that signified to me a frightening degree of helplessness, and one that came slowly to him. He had continued to work long after his hands were no longer functional, but it was only after his illness had forced his retirement from the law firm that he used the diagnostic term "quadriplegic" to refer to himself. I think it helped him admit the fact that MS had actually ended his working life. He was my only sibling. Mother was increasingly frail and diminished by senility. She often needed a wheelchair. My father had been dead for thirteen years. I had been healthy and active over the decades as Jeff's strong, athletic body became increasingly incapacitated and for some years was the only able-bodied member of my family. Lying in the hospital, I vaguely knew the word "quadriplegic" now applied to me, too, though my mind revolted from that likeness as a coincidence entirely too improbable to be true.

10

*

Violence
and the Sacred

As you know, Jeff was barely a year older than I, and, because I never had any interest in girls' sanctioned pastimes, I now and again imagined I was his twin. I didn't wish that I were a boy, and I don't remember this idea as a highly developed fantasy. It was rather an easy way to account for the fact that he and I dressed much alike and played together all the time. It was, of course, also a way to make sense of my competitiveness with him. After I started elementary school, when I got home I couldn't wait to change out of the dresses and skirts I had no choice but to wear, and into T-shirts and jeans. Dad taught us each to swim at the same time, in the lakes and dammed-up rivers we encountered when on camping trips, and would romp endlessly with us in the water. We both had baseball mitts, his with JEFF lettered in black magic marker on the wrist strap, mine with TINA, and Dad taught us both to throw. When Dad made slingshots for us using his jigsaw, I wood-burned TINA into mine and my brother burned JEFF into his. We made targets out of cans filled with stones, and would compete to see whose shots were the most deadly. A couple years later, Dad cut skateboards for us in his workshop downstairs, and helped us paint them with racing stripes. He then hacksawed roller skates in half and bolted the wheels to the boards. One summer we rode those boards every day. We shared baseballs and bats, and played tetherball out back for hours on end, or would shoot baskets and play H-O-R-S-E until it was too dark to see the rim. Downstairs in the basement we played epic matches of ping-pong on the table that Dad built. We were pretty evenly matched, in that as in most things. We both learned how to do the J-stroke when paddling in the stern of the canoe so as to keep it on course, and were directed by our parents to play fair and trade off who got to be in that coveted position. We played kick the can in the back yard with neighborhood kids, and "bicycle polo" with cobbled-together sticks and a tennis ball in an empty parking lot beside Oller Hall on the Juniata campus. We lived only a block away, and for us, the sidewalks, parking lots, paths, and athletic fields of the campus were all places to play. We played games of skill, coordination, strength, speed, and endurance all the time.

Our play was almost all physical, and almost always we were competing against each other. When we were bored in the car, we would play a reflex game Dad taught us. Jeff would reach out with palms up, I would reach out with palms down, over his hands but not touching. Then he would fast as lightning turn over his hand (or hands) to slap the top of mine. Sometimes he'd execute a successful fake to make me draw back needlessly, an error that exacted the penalty of a free slap. In time I would draw back without being touched, and then would be *my* turn to strike. We played until our hands were lobster red. Eventually the game would devolve into shoving and then to punching.

"That's *my* side of the seat." Jeff, incited to cross the line, put his hand over; I shoved him. He hauled off and punched me in the upper arm. "That hurt! Besides, I told you not to!" I hissed, and punched his thigh with my balled-up fist. Back and forth it would go, until the front seat noticed—on bad days, until Dad threatened to pull over and stop the car then and there. That quieted us down.

In nearly everything, Jeff and I were treated exactly the same. We were given the same allowance, starting at a quarter each week, supplemented by whatever 2¢ pop bottle deposits we could redeem, income and expenses both to be recorded every week on three-by-five index cards. In return for that allowance, we had the same household responsibilities. We alternated days "on call," when we had to be ready to run an errand to the little grocery store two blocks down the street, and were responsible for setting the table for dinner. When we were older, we had to clean our bedrooms before going out to play on Saturday.

If deeply aggrieved with each other, either one of us could "make a complaint" (so named to impress on us the gravity of "telling") to either Mother or Dad, who would be the final arbitrator of the dispute. Moreover, we learned that our family was a "company," with a single "company wallet" kept in a drawer by Mother's desk in the kitchen. Familial pedagogy encouraged us to understand ourselves as part of a democratic (albeit hierarchical) polity. The sway of reason was to prevail—that, I think, was my father's idea. For her part, Mother inculcated a feeling that was never articulated explicitly—as a family we were *always already* reconciled, strife among us banished by Christian forbearance and forgiveness. So we learned that conflict was to be avoided by submitting to reason and Christian love.

Yet Jeff and I fought all the time. We fought sometimes for fun, when we wrestled or pretended to box, and sometimes not, when we pummeled and pushed. Not every game devolved into fighting, but I do remember fighting all the time. Roughhousing often got serious, although even when we were outright fighting, there was an unspoken taboo against blows to the head or face. Hitting *hard* with a closed fist on any extremity we permitted. We really scrapped with each other, chasing through the house, banging doors and then wedging them shut with a foot, making a ruckus that could morph into real hostility. I think it likely that I was more often the aggressor. It is certain that I was bigger than Jeff from age two or three on. Not until he came back from his first year in college was he taller and decidedly stronger than I. Too often, strangers would assume that I, the girl, was the older one, a confusion that Jeff found truly hard to bear.

Moving through grade school, where I could never wear pants to school, even on the coldest days, I no longer felt so vividly my likeness to Jeff, but I think our family formation did much to keep that idea active in my unconscious life. At home we were treated alike, with no favoritism, and the communitarian ethos of church and college reinforced the familial ideal of equality that governed my parents' child rearing. We were given to understand that neither one of us had an advantage over the other. My idea that we could be taken for twins was, perhaps, a childish assertion of this logic when we were little. Jeff and I wore the same clothes, had the same equipment, played the same games, and were equally matched. What one was given, the other was given. Ergo, *we* were the same—as twins look to be. Because girls were deemed inferior to boys, I thereby claimed for myself the privileges of boyhood. Because my family was in some important ways eccentric, different in our often-articulated Anabaptist values from most families in our small, conservative central Pennsylvania town, I was praised for my physical abilities and aptitudes by parents who, thankfully, wanted to treat Jeff and me as junior partners in the Crosby Company. There's no way, however, to simply opt out of feeling the difference normative binary gender makes, and my father (more than my mother, I think) was troubled by the fact that I was physically bigger and more aggressive than Jeff—who was older and a boy. Certainly both Mother and Dad were annoyed, I imagine now and then even seriously troubled, by our constant pushing and shoving for whatever advantage was at hand. So at last there was a really big fight. There had to be.

Or so René Girard argues in his meta-psychological historical an-thropology, *Violence and the Sacred*, a book that makes several big claims and one small observation that has bearing here.[1] Girard is concerned with the way one act of violence incites another, and pos-its that the imposition of differential power is the only way to stop unending cycles of killing and revenge, each violent act replicating the one that had come before. In other words, likeness is a problem. "Wherever differences are lacking, violence threatens," he writes. "Order, peace, and fecundity depend on cultural distinctions; it is not these distinctions but the loss of them that gives birth to fierce rivalries." I think of the brothers of the Hebrew Bible—the murder-ous rivalry between Cain and Abel, or the struggle between the twins Esau and Jacob for preeminence and their father's blessing. Twins are especially to be feared as the "harbingers of indiscriminate violence." Perfect equilibrium can't be sustained and presages violence, thus justice requires an imbalance of power to create ethical distinctions. Only the introduction of some "transcendental quality" can bring an end to the cycle of vengeance by imposing a fundamental difference between the sanctioned violence of a judicial system and the unsanc-tioned violence of revenge.

* * *

In the last month of his life, as he was dying from prostate cancer, Dad spoke to his family, assembled around the kitchen table. He wanted to apologize, he began, for what happened that day long ago when he insisted that Jeff and I "fight it out." We both immediately assured him that the event was long lost in the mists of childhood and had left no psychic wounds, which on my part, at least, was more wishful than true. There in the kitchen, I remembered The Fight clearly enough, but was unable then to acknowledge even to myself the seriousness of the injury that was inflicted on me by my father and his son.

Here's what happened. Early one Saturday, Jeff and I were hanging out on the loveseat in Dad's study, which was downstairs and across the hall from the master bedroom (we were maybe eleven and ten years old?). Mother and Dad weren't up yet. I'll bet one of us said "Stop it! You're bugging me, so *keep off!*" We were pushing, shoving, and quarreling, when suddenly Dad stormed out of the bedroom—naked, as he slept naked—and dragged us both out into the living room. "If you're going to fight, fight it out," he shouted. "Fight it out, fight it out, fight till you're done." I can imagine few things more painful for Mother, who, wrapped in a bathrobe, was sobbing and kept pleading, "Ken, please stop, please stop." But there was no stopping the fight, which by now was serious as Jeff and I punched and grappled for advantage, really angry. I don't know how long the scrapping and hitting went on, nor do I remember any details about the fight except this. I was in retreat and tripped over the piano bench, then suddenly I was lying on my back and Jeff was on top of me, grabbing my shoulders and ready to bang my head against the floor (or had he already done so? maybe a couple times?). "Get off me! Get off!" I was crying, and finally, "I give up." The fight was over. As soon as I surrendered and Jeff let me up, I ran upstairs and locked the door to my bedroom. "Tina, Tina please come out. Tina, please talk to me. Come downstairs. Please," Mother repeatedly urged. But I refused to talk to her, and wouldn't even go near the door. Mother returned repeatedly, needing so deeply for all of us to forgive one another and be at peace. Not me. I wasn't unlocking that door, humiliated as I was, and I certainly wasn't ready for peace. I don't know how it was that I finally left the privacy of my room to rejoin the family.

* * *

Was it as I remember it? Was Dad really naked in this scene? That seems so—how shall I say it—Freudian. Did he really demand in so many words that we "fight it out," fight until his son was victorious? Until his daughter cried, "I give up"? Against his wife's tearful pleas? Who knows? Indeed, there's no knowing, and what matters, of course, is that this is the scene that I remember, and the scene that to the assembled family I declared long over and lost in the past. I now think differently. In that scene, Dad embodied the Law of the Father, in the psychoanalyst Jacques Lacan's phrase, that "transcendent quality" powerful enough to discriminate between twins, and separated us once and for all by asserting Jeff's difference from me, and his superiority as a boy. Certainly I felt that superiority as he straddled me, pinning me down and knocking me around. He was literally above me. When Dad finally couldn't stand the agonistic relationship between his children, and the ways in which I must've sometimes dominated Jeff, he established the (supposed) universal difference of a simple hierarchical binary, masculine over feminine, as it expresses the (supposed) foundational difference of sex, and mandated The Fight to sort out what was owing to his firstborn, his son.

Gender was in my father's hands—at that moment—a blunt instrument. Yet gender is, of course, not simply a matter of disciplining and punishing so as to create masculine boys and feminine girls. In fact, my parents supported me when I wanted clothing and toys not intended for girls. It was okay with them if I wanted "clodhopper" work boots, or high-top Converse All Stars, or cowboy boots and a jeans jacket, and they never tried to talk me out of playing sandlot football or baseball with the boys. They even gave me for my birthday present one year the toy rifle that I so longed for and knew, just *knew* that I wasn't going to get. They had little interest in conforming to the narrowly conservative social/political/ethical norms of our small town, and communicated that clearly enough to their children. Nonetheless, my tomboy resistance to girlhood was a complicated effort, and my parents, who let me dress and play as I wished, also mandated a femininity intended to distinguish me as a girl. I had long hair halfway down my back (though I always pulled it back into a tight ponytail), and I had, without exception, to wear dresses to church on Sunday.

* * *

The Fight, toward the end of elementary school, foreshadowed my trials in the gauntlet of puberty, where becoming normatively feminine meant carrying my books in front of me, instead of on my hip—one among many unspoken rules I encountered in seventh grade. *No one* rode a bicycle to school after sixth grade. With books stacked awkwardly before me, I would walk to school feeling my handbag slipping off my shoulder to my elbow, where it would bang against my leg and make a run in my nylons. Mother continued to wear her hair in the bob she had gotten in college, and was of little help to me in communicating the inside story of stylish femininity. My closest friends in junior high were two new girls who had gone to the other elementary school in Huntingdon, the one downtown. They were happy to shovel the snow off the school playground with me so that we could play basketball in winter, and they enjoyed playing pitch and catch as much as I did. Yet even they seemed to have the knack of femininity better than I, and by ninth grade each had the dubious success of a boyfriend. Gender was for me a kind of out-of-body experience, relieved only by playing varsity sports once I got to high school. Even there, femininity intruded—the field hockey uniform was a kilt, worn over black bloomers, and the basketball uniform a tunic belted in the middle, same bloomers. It didn't matter, however, because I was playing hard with my teammates, competing to win, and the uniforms had numbers, and everything! It's true that the girls' teams were called the "Huntingdon Bearkittens," while the boys were the "Huntingdon Bearcats," but I didn't care what we were called as long as we had girls' varsity sports. I do, however, regret chanting "Queer Grier Is Here" in the locker room before playing the team from the private Grier school for girls near Tyrone, long before "queer" was repurposed as a proud blazon.

* * *

There's a snapshot of Jeff and me that I've always liked. There we are, together on one side of the table, in front of a birthday cake covered with lit candles. Jeff turned twenty-one on August 13, 1973, the summer we were both working at the Brethren church camp near Huntington. My twentieth birthday was only three weeks later, so the cake may have been for both of us—that seems likely to me, since we were both going our separate ways at the end of August, and Mother sometimes combined our birthday celebrations when we were kids. That summer he was a counselor at Camp Blue Diamond, and I was the "waterfront director," a.k.a. the lifeguard, at the little lake, where I oversaw the beach and the swimming area, the canoes and the floating docks where they were moored. The color photo shows me deeply tan, and my hair, bleached blonde by the sun, is hanging in waves and curls down to my shoulders. I'm wearing big silver loop earrings. Jeff is also tan from his summer's work, and wears his brown, shoulder-length hair pulled back from his face in a ponytail. We are sitting side by side at the foldout teak table in the living room that Mother would set for festive events, and we're both smiling and looking at the camera. For decades I looked at this photo and thought we looked strikingly alike—the same blue eyes, strong nose, well-defined lips, clear jawline. Our smiles are much alike.

I found the photo in an album, got it out and put it in a wooden frame, and I see it now on top of a chest of drawers. I got it out because Jeff was gone and I wanted to be in his presence again. I mourned his death, and I mourned the life that he never got to lead, the one in which he didn't have MS, didn't endure the slow devastation of his body, and didn't end up paralyzed. The photo shows us in our youth, each strong in body after a summer at the camp. I had been swimming half a mile early every morning in the lake before climbing into the white lifeguard's chair, a slow crawl back and forth along the outer buoys. Jeff had hiked repeatedly to a fire tower on a nearby mountain, every week with a different group of campers, where they climbed the metal staircase all the way to the top to look out over the forested and farmland beauty of central Pennsylvania. There we are, both of us in great health, shining with potential, on the verge of full adulthood. Looking at this youthful birthday photo, it seems impossible that my vibrant, handsome brother would be stricken with a neurological disease that would bring him to quadriplegia in his forties, let alone that I would break my neck and at age fifty find myself quadriplegic, too.

One hot summer day, I was visiting Jeff, and we went out in his van to run errands. When we got back, I was lounging on a leather sofa that was cool to my cheek as I turned to look at Jeff sitting across from me in his wheelchair. How can he stand it, I wondered, always being in his wheelchair and never sprawled on the sofa? How can he stand never stretching his legs after a long drive? How can he stand going through the world so slowly, always having to wait for the lift to get into the van, never taking steps two at a time? How can he bear to live in a world so physically monotonous, with tactile sensation so dulled? How awful—to lose your grip and the use of your hands, literally lose your signature! A few years later, lying in my hospital bed, the thought came to me that I now had to answer those questions for myself. At the stroke of fifty, my fantasy of being Jeff's twin had been finally, malevolently realized. Paralysis trumped gender.

* * *

I remembered an essay by Freud that I had read long ago, "Das Unheimliche," or "The Uncanny." I was looking for anything to help me understand the particular fold in time I felt myself to be living in, a doubling back, terribly changed, to days long ago. Freud's essay treats the effects created by the horror stories of E. T. A. Hoffmann, a master of the genre, who often renders familiar domestic scenes creepy and threatening, as though through the looking glass. Something once familiar and safe becomes unfamiliar and unsettling—*unheimlich*, literally "un-homelike." Hoffman creates a kind of doubtful suspense about what's really happening by introducing some form or another of a shadow figure, a doppelgänger, or by describing a setting that you immediately recognize as every day . . . but now it's off-kilter, and populated with frightening characters. The walking dead, ghosts, and zombies are creatures of horror both alive and dead, but even more frightening are the familiars who intrude into what should be ordinary everyday life, bringing with them a whiff of the underworld. A soldier missing and presumed dead returns, but his loved ones are incapable of recognizing him, or a familiar domestic world is not right, somehow, an oddness all the more threatening because barely perceptible, yet unmistakably there. Episodes of *The Twilight Zone* are often of this sort, and Edgar Allen Poe's horror stories sometimes work by the same logic.

Freud introduces his study of the *unheimlich* with an analysis of its opposite, *heimlich*, or homelike, homey. We discover with surprise a fact that Freud finds quite significant—the word contains *within itself* its own antonym. *Heimlich* means both familiar, homey, and comfortable, *and also* that which is concealed, out of sight or hidden in the home, thereby transforming the family home into a place of threatening secrets. *Heimlich* and *unheimlich* tell the same story. "[E]verything is uncanny that ought to have remained secret and hidden, and yet comes to light." The *unheimlich* "leads back to something long known to us, once very familiar," but only through an analysis that, as it were, raises the dead.[2] For Freud, the *unheimlich* is illustrative of mental life. You consciously admire yourself as a rational, civilized creature, yet all the while repressed thoughts literally too repulsive and ugly to be acknowledged profoundly affect how you live your life. Unbeknownst to you, you're a double agent. The unconscious gathers to it all that must be forgotten and remain beyond conscious reflection if orderly adult life is to be achieved and preserved.

I don't want to pursue here an orthodox Freudian analysis, but I am convinced that child rearing inevitably creates thoughts that are unthinkable, and that later reappear in a different guise in dreams and fantasies. My father apparently needed his son to fight and win, and my loving mother loved me perhaps not wisely, but too well. As a friend of mine observed when we were talking about her soon-to-be adolescent son, she'd come to understand that all she could do was her best, and that it would be his job to sort it all out for himself later on. I want to be very clear, my parents and my brother did their very best by me, and I by them. I loved my family when I was a child, and I love them now. Nonetheless. Of these matters Philip Larkin writes,

THIS BE THE VERSE

They fuck you up, your mum and dad.
    They may not mean to, but they do.
    They fill you with the faults they had
    And add some extra, just for you.

But they were fucked up in their turn

. . .

The crude Anglo-Saxon energy of "fuck" extends through the poem's three stanzas, which sustain unmodulated the tension of the first line—your parents "fuck you up" both literally and metaphorically, bringing you into this world only to leave you damaged. The harsh language posits this damage as existential, the unavoidable pain of human being declared in two simple, short declarative sentences. Tetrameter reinforces the crude language with the four-beat line of traditional ballad, nursery rhyme, and popular music, and the rhythm is relentlessly enforced by the insistently monosyllabic words of the first two stanzas. "Ex´ tra" is the sole exception—an extra syllable, as it were, to assert that "you" inherit your parents' faults, and then some.

The inevitability of damage extends generationally as the poem moves into the compound-complex sentence that makes up its second stanza. It begins, "But they were fucked up in their turn," and continues not by excusing the parents for their fucked-up parenting, but by committing the poem to an increasingly bleak, multigenerational view. The meter continues to be unrelentingly blunt. When I first read the poem, I was in analysis, and I knew it was addressed to me. "This Be the Verse" told me that all families are fucked up, and suggested to me that the representation of happy families everywhere you turn may be compensation for unavoidable pain. "This Be the Verse" in its existential bleakness spoke so immediately to me because I was trying to figure out how I could have suffered in the intimacy of my loving family—an intimacy that depended on suppressing hostility, which made it impossible to declare and work through anger, envy, greed, lust, sloth—the whole catalog of mortal and venial sins. Larkin's arresting, generative obscenities are harsh, and seem to have no application to my loving family. Yet I've committed the poem to memory and could recite it to you now.

The third and final stanza summarizes the existential drama of being fucked up with a significant change in diction.

> Man hands on misery to man.
> It deepens like a coastal shelf.
> Get out as early as you can,
> And don't have any kids yourself.[3]

The poem arrives at the grand abstraction "Man," and the three Anglo-Norman syllables of "mi´ ser y." The tone of the poem becomes formal. Misery deepens through simile, which brings us to the final two lines, an enjambed imperative. Unlike my friend, who has both a daughter and a son, the speaker of the poem has no wish to "fuck up" a child, in either meaning of that verb. In his world, there's no having a child without in some way royally fucking things up. I'm of a generally optimistic temperament, but in this case I'm with the speaker—I have no kids myself.

I've come to think that the happiness my mother and father enjoyed in their marriage may have led them to believe that their way of life was not simply the best for *them*, but the best for *everyone* and the only way to live a fulfilling life. We didn't keep good track of photographs as I was growing up, but there is a white album with a series of pictures taken the day of their wedding. One is a candid snapshot taken in between the formal posed photographs. They are standing facing each other, with their heads thrown back in laughter, as Jane is reaching out for Ken's hand. At some point Mother annotated the picture—"Joy, Joy, Joy! Here we are!" So they were, and I'm happy for them every time I look at it. I believe they delighted in each other, but pumped the air out of the room for me.

I can imagine how much parents must hope for the well-being of their children, so I was not surprised when my father told me on the eve of his son's wedding that he hoped that I, too, would marry and "in due course" have children. I was dead certain neither acts were in my future. Jeff and I had both just graduated from college, and I had been with my family for two days in Rochester, New York, doing the things that you do before a wedding. Earlier that day I had suddenly bolted out of Beth's parents' house after Mother had me try on the bridesmaid's dress she was sewing to check where it should be hemmed. It was a gown of blue sprigged muslin with short puff sleeves that, given the way I carry myself, made me look like a linebacker. I wandered, crying hard and surprised by my emotion, around the suburban sameness of a neighborhood that defied my best efforts to distinguish among its streets. I am quite sure that I didn't think *that* much about the gown, and I don't remember coming to any conclusions about my misery. In retrospect, the weekend of the wedding is all affect—a profound, mute feeling of unbelonging that I couldn't admit even to myself. I certainly didn't want to marry, and still don't—it's a contract filed with and enforced by the state, which proceeds to dole out social goods with reference to that bond. It's a tie that binds women to domestic labor, the infamous, unpaid "second shift" that so many women begin when they get home from the factory, or the office, or the restaurant where they've been waiting on people all day. Why the hell would I want to marry?

All this went unsaid. Given the indirection our family practiced, perhaps it's no wonder that when Jeff and I were kids both our play and our disagreements were fiercely physical. I'm sure I wanted to take his place and the nebulous privileges he enjoyed as the son who was the firstborn—older than me, but just barely, and not as big. I know for sure that he felt bad about that. A real struggle for precedence motivated the competition we elaborated over the years. All that faded into the background as we got older, and I found my own sense of self in lesbian-feminism. He was twenty-one when he married, and I had not yet reached that auspicious age. I remember thinking there goes the golden boy, as he and Beth drove away towing a small U-Haul trailer full of wedding gifts—curious, because I truly didn't want all that stuff. To the contrary, I was happy that everything I owned, including my stereo speakers, could fit in a VW bug. In August 1974 I believed that I didn't care about the fact that the whole wedding thing made very much of him and very little of me. I now think that I both did and did not want what he had, a flat-out contradiction in the light of reason, but perfectly consistent with unconscious thought and unavowed feelings. The roiling, unconscious underside of family life is beyond the reach of reason.

Jeff did well in law school, passed the bar exam, and became a lawyer. He and Beth started a family. And then, as I neared the end of graduate school, the terrible fact of MS and its multiplying sclerotic destruction of myelin laid him low. The competition that had structured our relationship, both for good and ill, was suddenly over, and I was the winner, by default.

That's ludicrous, of course, but I guess that's my point—MS separated Jeff from me more profoundly than gender, and that's saying a lot. I didn't want to win that way, if I wanted to "win" at all. There was no joy in such a triumph, yet I can't help but think I must have felt guilty as the fit and flourishing one. The difference between us was more and more evident every time I visited. Every time the intervening months had worked their changes. Perhaps that made me more attached to the idea that there was a strong family resemblance between us, the similarity that I saw so clearly in the birthday photograph. I could hold onto that. That photo had always made me happy, in part, surely, because I saw him as a handsome man and enjoyed the reflected glory. I was sad to see the changes in his body as the muscles in his legs began to atrophy, his torso muscles weakened, and he slowly lost his upright posture. The sicker he got, the more different from me he was, the more I wished I could help him. The more I wished he were like me.

Alas, no. We were not twins, mirroring each other in an eternal likeness, and never had been. Our lives had taken different trajectories, which continued even after I broke my neck. At first, Jeff and I would sit together in our wheelchairs. Before long, however, the labor of getting up became too much for him, so snapshots show me in my chair beside his hospital bed. He remained, despite these changes, such an alive person that it never occurred to me his death could be imminent. The shock of that event seems to have decisively changed how I see Jeff, and I mean that quite literally. We were always more different than my unconscious mind would admit. I couldn't see it while he was alive, but evidence of that difference is right there in the birthday photograph. We don't look uncannily alike. No. Our facial features are very similar, but not the structure of our faces. My face is rounder (like Mother's), while his is more angular (like Dad's). There's a strong family resemblance, that's all.

* * *

My mother died in October 2008. We waited until a beautiful day in July 2009 to scatter her ashes at the Peace Chapel at Juniata, which was designed by Maya Lin, the site-specific architect who designed the Vietnam War Memorial in Washington, D.C. You go up an unmarked dirt road climbing through woods that open out to a field on the knoll of a hill. Grasses and wildflowers have been cut in a large circle, and at the center there's a smaller circle about twenty feet in diameter excavated a yard deep. The grass inside is mowed near to the ground. This grassy interior is lined with a circle of granite blocks flush to the earth, which invite you to sit down to take in the tranquil woods and mountains in the middle distance. Summer insects buzz in the grasses, and you can hear birds calling in the woods. A wide path mowed through grasses and wildflowers, and laid with large, smooth granite steppingstones set some distance apart, runs uphill and into the trees. Up there you can find a granite disk set flush with the ground, making a place for private meditation that's spatially connected to the circle below. When we scattered Kenneth Ward Crosby's ashes one May dawn in 1990, Mother said that he was "universalized," and I ran, crying, alone up the hill and into the woods to find that stone in the still light of the very early morning. The whole of the chapel is very simple and very beautiful. Jane Miller Crosby's molecules are now mingled with the air, soil, and water of the place that years earlier accepted what remained of her dear Ken. The last time I spoke face to face with Jeff and enjoyed his presence was on that warm July day the family gathered to remember Mother, and commend what remained of her body to the elements. A year later, the family took a portion of Jefferson Clark Crosby's ashes to be blown by the breezes and disappear into the grasses on the same peaceful hillside looking out to the Appalachian mountain ridges running off into the distance. I don't know when I will next go to Huntingdon, though I'm sure I will, drawn there by Kathy, who for many years worked as Mother's aide, and became her loving—and much loved—companion. The memories of my family will also urge me to return. I'm so vividly aware of how much I love them, which has confused me, given the distance I took. Jane, Ken, and Jeff are gone. I draw close to them in my memories with no reserve, and see them anew. I am not Jeff's twin. I don't even resemble him as much as I had thought. That revelation helps me to see him more as he was—and is yet another loss.

11

✳

Bowels Lead

"I've got to get to the bathroom. Now." Jeff spoke with real urgency as he pivoted his wheelchair away from the kitchen table where we were sitting drinking coffee after breakfast. "I hardly ever drink coffee—it can be a problem for me—makes me need to move my bowels," he anxiously explained as he rolled down the hall. The MS was robbing him of sphincter control, and Janet and I shared his anxiety about getting him onto the toilet in time. I positioned myself behind him, grabbed him under his armpits, Janet got his knees, and we did our best to boost him onto the toilet. As it turned out, his bowels let loose just as he got his pants down and began to transfer, so by the time he was actually on the toilet, he'd made a real mess. Shit on his underwear and jeans, shit on the floor, shit smeared all over the toilet seat. Not much in the toilet. "I'm so sorry," he repeatedly said with frustrated anger. Then more calmly, "Sorry about the cleanup. I *hate it* when this happens. *Hate it.* What a mess! This is why I've been thinking about a bowel program, but once you start, that's it."

I was really focused on reassuring him that I didn't mind cleaning up his shit, so I didn't ask what he meant by "bowel program." I had no idea, and I certainly didn't want to imagine having to embrace further decline, so didn't stop to ask. At that moment, I had to get his pants and his underwear off, rinse off the worst of the shit in the shower, and then give the clothing to Janet to throw in the washing machine. I was busy wiping up the floor, the toilet, and Jeff's bottom, as best I could. While it truly was a mess, I didn't mind cleaning up because I loved Jeff. It only saddened me that the MS made his life so hard. At forty-eight years old, here he was revisiting the toilet training that we passed through as toddlers on our way to becoming adults. Mother used to rinse out our soiled diapers in the toilet before washing them, I thought, as I helped him pull on fresh underwear and clean jeans. Here his bowels are once again unreliable and sometimes out of his control. I can't imagine living as he does, I thought to myself, I really can't.

The "bowel program" remained vague to me, since I never really inquired into what the phrase meant. So I don't actually know when he started to use laxatives and enemas to regulate the passing of stool from his body. It wasn't until I was introduced to *my* bowel program in the rehab hospital that I came to understand what Jeff faced. The MS first disabled his legs, then his hands and arms and the muscles of his torso, and slowly eroded the neural circuits governing his organs. Years ago, he slowly stopped singing as he could no longer project the air strongly enough from his lungs to produce his lovely baritone. I worried about the future, which held the certainty of ever decreasing lung function, the threat of aspirating food, the horror of a respirator. His bowels began imperceptibly, and then more evidently to slow down, until he needed more than the erratic stimulation of coffee to stir them into motion. By the time he was living in a nursing unit of the Moravian Manor, he was wholly dependent on an every-other-day program of laxatives followed by an enema—the laxatives given the night before, the enema on the day of the bowel program itself. The nurse would turn him over, insert an enema into his anus, squeeze it into his rectum, and then turn him back over onto a bed pan. The chemicals would work in about thirty minutes, and he would passively move his bowels—he could no longer "push." Then a nurse would roll him slightly off the bed pan, so as to insert a gloved finger into his anus to check for any stool that remained. If she felt something, she would move her finger in a rapid circular motion to manually stimulate the muscles of the rectum and create the contractions necessary to empty out completely.

"Bowels lead." I don't know where I picked up this phrase, but its two-word simplicity states a simple truth. Maggie's grandfather was a dentist who would dismiss his granddaughters' complaints of discomfort by saying, "If you don't have a fever and you're moving your bowels, you're fine." True enough—failure to get rid of your body's waste will certainly kill you. But what about all the suffering in between, now diminished into nothingness by this dismissively hyperbolic comparison? My bowels are moving, my temperature's normal, but I'm far from fine, because my bowels are now a great mental, emotional, and physical trouble to me. In fact, my own bowel program sometimes horrifies me—it's *mine*, it's unavoidable, unpleasant, and sometimes downright nasty. What troubles me most, however, is a simple fact—I'll never *not* have an insistent and unforgettable bowel program in my insistent, unforgettable future. The future of my body can only be worse than it is now.

Of course, any bowel "mistake" is deeply embarrassing—just ask the toddler who has successfully graduated from diapers, but has somehow inadvertently dumped in his pants. Further, who among us has not released upon the world a quiet, evil-smelling fart and then pretended to know nothing about it? As you know, even before my spinal cord was injured, I suffered from intestinal gas. One day when Janet and I were driving a U-Haul from Arizona to Connecticut we stopped in a McDonald's for coffee, and I quietly farted the world's worst fart when paying at the cash register. The woman serving me glanced around and then said to no one in particular, "What's that horrible smell? Yuck—it smells like something's rotten or dead." Believe me, I wasn't owning up to that mortification! I'll bet that you can think of at least one similar disavowal of passed gas, though perhaps not as dramatic. But unless you, too, are living with partially paralyzed bowel muscles (or are caring for someone so paralyzed), I doubt you know any more than I did about bowel function and paralysis before I broke my neck.

Jeff no longer moves his bowels. He's dead. I, however, am very much alive and move my bowels on an unvarying schedule: two days off, three capsules of a powerful herbal laxative and stool softener on the evening of the second, followed by a morning enema on the third day, then an hour or two—or even, at the very worst, three—sitting over the toilet, with digital stimulation when I think I'm done. That's when everything's going well. Sometimes everything doesn't go well. In the past year I've twice suffered through the second day feeling real heaviness in my bowels, which gathered into a near certainty that I had to go—NOW. I had hoped to get through the night, but no. Both times I've had to ask for help around midnight, once rousting Donna from her sleep and once delaying Janet's bedtime with me. No one was in bed before 2:30 A.M., because I shower after my time on the toilet. I can feel my sphincter muscle, and flex it—as I can feel and flex all my muscles—but it's not innervated enough to stop any stool that's on the way out. You can't imagine how helpless I feel.

One of the most significant victories a young child wins, for which she is trained and praised, is control of her bowels. Sphincter control matters, as does the ability to "push." Here's what happens when you have a bowel movement:

> When the rectum is filled, pressure within it is increased. This increased intrarectal pressure initially forces the walls of the anal canal

apart and allows the fecal material to enter the canal; as material is entering, muscles attached to the pelvic floor help further to pull the anal canal walls apart. The rectum shortens as it expels material into the anal canal, and peristaltic waves propel the feces out of the rectum. In the anus there are two muscular constrictors, the internal and external sphincters, that allow the feces to be passed or retained. As feces exit, the anus is drawn up over the passing mass by muscles of the pelvic diaphragm to prevent prolapse (pushing out of the body) of the anal canal.[1]

This complicated process is what we ask all toddlers to control, using the euphemism of "accident" to name any failure. The child nonetheless knows that an accident is not neutral, but is rather her responsibility, to be chalked up to her account. Freud emphasizes this understanding and the slowly advancing control the child gains. Indeed, psychoanalytic theory goes further back still, to the raw "hommelette," in Lacan's play on words, the unformed infant whose brain is still growing when she is born, and whose cranium is not yet whole, who slowly, slowly grows up being handled—being cooked, as it were—by adults. Her body is repeatedly marked out for her nascent contemplation by the special attention given to all of her orifices. The child successfully trained to use the toilet is on her way to understanding the adult world and its mysterious imperatives and rewards.

*   *   *

Writing these details, I'm reminded of the pregnant phrase "too much information." Indeed. Yet as you know, a good bowel movement can be a real satisfaction, even if we don't discuss moving our bowels in polite company. W. H. Auden, despite this conversational norm, wrote a ten-stanza poem about that pleasure, "The Geography of the House," and dedicated it to his friend and sometime lover Christopher Isherwood. He begins with the fact that we all feel better when our bowels are regular, saying that we should "Raise a cheer to Mrs. / Nature for the primal / Pleasure She bestows." As the poem progresses, the speaker arrives at the psychoanalytic insight that links the work of toilet training with adult creativity.

> Lifted off the potty,
> Infants from their mothers
> Hear their first impartial
> Words of worldly praise:
>
> . . .
>
> All the arts derive from
> This ur-act of making,
> Private to the artist:
> Makers' lives are spent
> Striving in their chosen
> Medium to produce a
> De-narcissus-ized en-
> During excrement.

The poem continues to gather in consequence as it nears the end.

> Global Mother, keep our
> Bowels of compassion
> Open through our lifetime,
> Purge our minds as well:
> Grant us a king ending,

Not a second childhood,
Petulant, weak-sphinctered,
In a cheap hotel.

Auden understands that the phrase "Bowels of compassion" renders
a merciful and generous emotion visceral and deeply, internally felt,
while the poem itself embodies generosity. "Mrs. / Nature" becomes
humanity's "Global Mother," who compassionately endows with
pleasure a function necessary to life. He develops exfoliative ramifications from this unsung, lifelong pleasure, and links it to creativity
itself. Every time you "go" after breakfast you (unconsciously) recall
the satisfaction of making something that pleased your earliest caretaker, and all artists hope to create a "De-narcissus-ized en- / During
excrement," a thing made with another in mind, so that it can be
truly valued by others. The poem happily reminds its readers that
the m/other-directed pleasure of controlling our bowels motivates
"All the arts," because artistic creation is profoundly reliant upon the
unconscious bodily life of the artist. The speaker goes on to petition
the Global Mother for an old age free of bowel incontinence, and
links that failure of control to an impoverished life. Then his final
stanza returns to the present moment and the "primal pleasure" of
the poem's opening:

Mind and Body run on
Different timetables:
Not until our morning
Visit here can we
Leave the dead concerns of
Yesterday behind us,
Face with all our courage
What is now to be.[2]

The poet turns to the future, and the infinitive "to be" brings his poem to an end. Auden leaves readers with the verb of being—I am, you are, s/he is. We are, you are, they are. Quite truly, bowels lead.

No wonder Jeff didn't want to lose control over his bowels— moving your bowels is about life itself. If you read the label on any laxative or enema, you'll be warned off regular use, because the chemicals, whether plant derived or lab produced, will take over. You'll lose the ability to move waste through your system and out of your body, and become dependent upon the chemical stimulation. If central nervous system damage has brought you to your bowel program, getting an enema and then sitting on the commode will become part of your routine of care, with no end other than death in sight. It makes sense that Jeff wanted to avoid reliance on chemicals as long as he could. In time, though, he had more and more accidents like the one I helped to clean up. He became "weak-sphinctered," and needed to make a change.

Jeff clearly experienced the need to decide on a bowel program as a qualitatively different sort of change from the many other adaptive choices he had made through the years. When he could no longer reliably push his self-propelled wheelchair, he joked that he "couldn't wait to get the electric chair." The dark underside of his phrase acknowledged a loss, but the power chair itself enhanced his life. It was more comfortable, with better support for his body, and it sure was fast. He soon mastered the joystick, and loved making me run to keep up. The bowel program, on the other hand, was no joking matter. Its arrival announced only loss.

I wish now that Jeff and I had talked more about his feelings about his body, especially after he retired. On the rebound from his divorce, he started a relationship that worked for a while, but pretty quickly deteriorated. For a couple of years before my accident, we

spent a lot of time talking about that stalled relationship as he struggled on in the ever more aggravating, repetitive quarrel he and his
lover elaborated. One thread was conversation about the future. She
would pessimistically imagine for him a rapid physical decline that
was at odds with his own inherently more optimistic view of life, and
he confided in me their increasing, iterative, and exhausting disagreements. But we spent little to no time discussing how relentless illness
and gathering incapacity *feel.* Then I broke my neck, and when I
was again able to closely attend to my brother, he had moved to the
nursing home. I was awake to the horror of our twinning each other
in paralysis, and feared that we would soon talk only about the daily,
intimate care serious paralysis demands—how hard it is to set up
that care, how hard it is sometimes to receive. I swore I would never
talk with him about his bowel program or mine, would say nothing
about his catheter or mine, his urinary tract infections or mine, his
Foley bag or mine. Let alone about how I felt about my new relation
to shit and piss.

Then six months before he died, he sent me an e-mail saying that
he was having trouble, too often completing his routine of laxative
and enema only to shit in the bed, or even worse, shit after he was
up. Getting up and dressed was becoming increasingly onerous for
him and certainly for his aides, so to soil his pants and the cushion of
his chair shortly after he was positioned there was deeply frustrating
to him. All that work to get dressed and in his chair, only to make a
mess! He wondered how my bowel program went. So I told him all
about it, and we talked over the terrible fact that, unlike me, he could
no longer push at all to move stool through the anal canal. Toward
the end of his life, only the chemicals of an enema and digital stimulation could clear waste from his body, and sometimes that simply
wasn't enough. So we did, in the end, discuss in some detail both his
bowel program and mine.

* * *

When Janet and I arrived at Moravian Manor to visit Jeff on New Year's Eve 2009, we came with funny hats and noisemakers, ready to celebrate with him the arrival of 2010, and planning a New Year's Day packed with football watching. His physician would write a prescription for a six-pack when his book club was coming over, so we had bought both popcorn and beer. We got a terrible shock. We didn't expect to see any other family members when we arrived, but we turned the corner to find Kirsten running down the hall after toddler Justin, who was always on the move. She was crying hard, and sobbed to us, "Jeff is dying. He's dying of congestive heart failure. The nurse just told us."

I couldn't believe it. His move to the nursing home decisively broke off his already broken relationship, which enabled a significant rapprochement with Beth. She had called us two days earlier to let us know that he might have a urinary tract infection, and that he was taking antibiotics as he had done so many times in the past and sleeping a lot. There had never before in his life been any talk about heart trouble, so I didn't understand what Kirsten was telling me. Driving to Lancaster, I fully expected him to recover from the infection, as did we all. Urinary tract infections are old and familiar antagonists to anyone wearing a catheter. Besides, Jeff had been strong enough to join the family twice for Christmas celebrations just a few days earlier. A little further back, in mid-December, he had sent out his annual holiday letter in which he spoke of the future with no hint that he mightn't see the coming months. Later, after Kirsten had time to think over the previous couple of days, she said that he had almost certainly aspirated some beer during Christmas dinner, when drinking from a bottle she was holding for him—suddenly he jerked away and tried to cough, but his diaphragm was no longer innervated enough, so he sat at the table gasping for breath.

Now, when we walked into his room, he was lying propped up in the bed, already unable to speak, laboring for breath, his blue eyes moving from one face to another. How could he possibly be dying, and only communicating with his eyes? We spoke to him, touched him, told him how much we loved him, but he couldn't reply. He had been coherent and talking so very recently! That morning! Months later, Elaine, who worked as a nurse before getting her Ph.D. in English, helped me understand how the fatally compromised muscle that was his heart could not circulate enough oxygenated blood, and his body needed all the energy it could summon just to keep breath moving in and out. That's why speech had quickly become impossible. Earlier that day, when it was clear to the nursing staff that he was rapidly worsening, his physician had been called to his bedside and was able to put the question directly to Jeff. "Do you want under any circumstance to go to the hospital?" Jeff quite clearly said, "No." That clarity was consistent with the end-of-life directives he had drawn up earlier, and relieved all of us from wondering about medical decisions regarding the level of care he wanted. When he said "no," he knew he was refusing heroic measures that he didn't want to keep him alive.

Poor Colin had gotten the call that his father was dying, and was driving up from Baltimore. He arrived to kiss Jeff and tell him he loved him, and to watch with the rest of us Jeff's excruciatingly labored breathing. How long could he possibly last, working so hard to breathe? The New Year turned as I spent the night in my chair next to Jeff's bed and Janet sat beside me. We leaned on each other with our eyes closed, while Kirsten and Colin slept uneasily on mats in the physical therapy room, and Beth dozed on blankets spread on the floor at the foot of his bed. Janet and I left for the hotel early in the morning, only to find a poignant reminder of the visit that we had imagined—hats, noisemakers, and complimentary champagne in an ice bucket, the ice long since melted. When I was able to gather myself and reflect, I realized that the information he had given me about his bowel program several months earlier was evidence that his body was truly shutting down, a process now impossibly speeded up, so that when Janet and I came to his bedside again later that morning, his eyes were open but unseeing.

His impaired circulation was slowly depriving his whole body of life. Breathing became increasingly difficult, until every breath he drew gurgled through thick mucus that just kept coming and coming, at times pouring out of his mouth and nose—the congestion of congestive heart failure. Once or twice a respiratory therapist suctioned mucus out of his throat and lungs, but it made little difference, since his body only produced more. Even now, the bowel program obtruded, for it is nothing if not relentless. Medical protocol dictates that a patient may delay a bowel program for no more than a certain number of shifts, a nurse informed us when she came in with an enema. It is, however, within your power to refuse medical advice, which Kirsten did, backed by his living will. So he was spared that last iteration of the bowel program, though his dying took four days. He always had one of the family with him, and many friends stopped to embrace him one last time. There was much singing of hymns and much praying. I was so heartbroken at his suffering that I at one point looked up from my vigil by his head and said, crying, "Pam, would you please pray?" I asked her for prayer because she was Jeff's pastor, and I desperately needed the assurance he was being carried through the crisis. I was utterly at a loss. Kirsten and Colin cycled through the playlist on his computer, keeping the music he loved playing for him, while the high-end Logitech computer speakers I'd bought him for Christmas sat unnoticed on the floor, wrapped in colorful paper and tied with a bow. The staff of Moravian Manor set up a folding table in the corridor outside his room that was soon covered with food, as in long-ago covered-dish dinners at the Stone Church of the Brethren that I attended as a child, but there was no pleasure in any of it. I'm still troubled by my memories of his death, which seemed to me like a slow drowning, though I've been assured that the Ativan and the morphine pump implanted midway through the process eased his way. It still breaks my heart.

Mind and body do, indeed, "run on different timetables." Jeff remains very much in mind, despite the fact that his body is now gone, some of his ashes buried in a memorial garden at his church and some scattered into the grasses of the Peace Chapel. That portion of his bodily remains has been taken by the winds, and driven by the rain into the ground, into the streams, out to sea, and who knows where. No doubt Jeff remains in my body. Surely he lives on in the brokenness of my bowels and the brokenness of my heart. I carry memories of him in other parts of my body, too, happy memories of childhood play running, riding, jumping, turning, catching, throwing, hitting, aiming and releasing, grappling and letting go. Maybe remembering Jeff also helps me somehow to endure my quadriplegic body. I couldn't imagine what it was like to live as Jeff did before I got hurt, and I know I can't always comprehend what it is to live as I do now, yet I live on. The bowels lead for life, to the release of "a satisfactory / Dump," as Auden imagines, and although the pleasure of that "dump" is forever gone out of my life, my bowels still evacuate waste. Although I thought I never would, I wrote to Jeff describing my bowel movements, and he replied. This correspondence was a practical exchange about a function necessary to life, and was in no way elevated. The poet would have approved, for he writes, "When we seem about to / Take up Higher Thought / Send us some deflating / Image like the pained ex / pression on a Major / Prophet taken short." Auden's image should ironize any happy idea that disability leads to profound insight or higher understanding, despite the narrative arc that organizes so many stories about living with an incapacitated bodymind. That arc carries the troubled subject through painful trials to livable accommodations and lessons learned, and all too often sounds the note triumphant. Don't believe it. Much of how I live, especially the working of my bowels, is simply beyond belief.

12

*

I'm Your
Physical Lover

When Maggie walked into the hospital room, she said, "You're beautiful." I didn't believe her, but I loved her for saying it, nonetheless.
Nine years earlier, she had been my student, and now we were friends.
I read her books of poetry as she began to publish, and felt deep satisfaction as she made her way to success as a writer. When I got to the
rehab hospital, she started driving every other weekend up to Middletown from New York City, where she repeatedly borrowed a car so
as to come to my side. Janet needed time away from the hospital, so
Maggie would spell her on the weekends, staying with me Saturday
afternoons and Sunday mornings. She moved to Middletown to teach
for a year at Wesleyan, and was here to help and to support us for
months and months after I came home. In that time, she, too, suffered, and endured the unbecoming that is the blank sign of a deeply
felt love betrayed. I loved Maggie before the accident, and two years
of intensely heightened intimacy profoundly confirmed that love. She
is a writer and a teacher, and in that time we talked about a world of
things—sex, desire, bodies, heartbreak, language, love, poetry. I was
devastated with pain. Neurological destruction made a wilderness of
my body. I was in an agony of grief. Being Maggie's friend in this time
took me out of myself, and I will be forever grateful.

In this passage from a long (six-page) lyric poem addressed to me, "Halo Over the Hospital," she represents one of our exchanges in the rehab hospital. (The halo was made by the brilliant yellow leaves of the trees around the building that were illuminated by the sun one day in November 2003.)

> Later I sit on the bed
> and tell you a little about my spastic love-life, about the person
> I'm trying not to be in love with
> You ask if we went home and fucked, I say we did
> and you are happy, and I love the way the word *Fuck*
> comes out of your wired mouth, as if desire can never be
> closed down or tortured out, as if *Fuck* will always bubble out
> of a metal forest. I tell you a little more
> and you say, *Good for fucking, bad for future planning*
> You say I don't have to be ashamed of my desire
> Not for sex, not for language
> You say that you learned by age 50
> that you need them both, together, and that you and J have that.
> You've been so happy. Crying now you say
> *All I can think is that if we built it once*
> *we can build it again* and I know you will and tell you so . . .

The idea of fucking still makes me happy—its Anglo-Saxon frankness is closer, I think, to the pleasures of sex than the anodyne phrase "making love," and the possessive register of "having sex" is all wrong. It has you as much as you have it.

Janet and I did once again build a durable life bridging swift and treacherous currents. Irremediable grief remains, however, a still powerful force, and I feel its deep tug every day. For me, fucking is so changed from what it was that, try as I may, I cannot reconcile myself to my losses. How can I settle for a life with deadened sensation that decrees I'll never again have an orgasm? How can I live on with profoundly compromised strength and tactile perception, especially in my hands? How I miss the way sex used to feel! How I miss feeling my entire body—every molecule, every atom, every subatomic particle, every Higgs boson—moved by desire! My hands used to be strong and capable, and I used them to good purpose in sex. No more. Nor can I move my body with any ease or pleasure. I can't even roll over in bed! I have to pull myself into a sitting position, cross one leg over the other, look back over the opposite shoulder, reach that arm backward at extension to support my weight, and with my other arm hook my crossed leg at the knee to draw it toward me, which will turn my hips as I lie back down.

I feel my losses so acutely because Janet and I enjoyed a sex life (love that phrase) that was really thrilling. For quite some time after we became lovers, we kept the futon down in the living room, rather than having it masquerade as a sofa, because we so often turned to fucking as we would talk, read, or watch football on TV. Thrills are a kind of peak intensity, and it's true that "futon living," as we called it, couldn't go on forever. After a while, we returned the furniture to its more public posture. The real thrill, however, was unabated, and that was the exciting possibility of an ever renewable resource, always available to us, an affirmation of intertwined and amplifying love and desire.

when you open your eyes, . . . you're slightly stricken
upon remembering the prison
your body has become. *I'm frightened,* you say
Then *I'm sad, so sad to be paralyzed,* and I'm sad too
You can't wipe away your tears because your hands
don't move, and I can't wipe them away either

because it's too abrupt a motion, everything now
needs to happen very slowly. So we place
a wet towel across your eyes and the tears
must soak upwards . . .

Everyone at home wants to know if you are OK
You're not "OK," you're paralyzed and in tremendous pain
Everyone keeps asking, *do you think she will walk again?*
But that really isn't the issue . . .
Apparently the spine runs the bowels and the blood
and just about everything else, miraculous and hurt
jelly cord. Your whole body suddenly withered and transparent
We can see your muscles move with the electrodes on
you have some tricep, no bicep, your left quad jerked
but no luck on the right[1]

Maggie's words recall to me so clearly my condition in the hospital,
and make present once again the physical incapacity, unfocused fear,
and infinite sadness of those months. How could I be this body? How
could I bear what I had become? How live with this soul-destroying
pain? How could I ever be desirable to someone else, when my body
so confused and frightened me?

From the first, I had sensation from the soles of my feet to the
top of my head. The further up my body, the clearer the sensation.
My face, for instance, registered everything as it used to do, despite
the arch bars, but my hands were quite another story, curled into
loose fists that I could not open. Fingertips that once could deli-
cately, precisely stroke a lover's clit and register her every response,
and fingers that could fill her vagina were now disabled and their
sensitivity deadened. Janet would sit on a chair pulled close to the
bed, and would sometimes open her hand and press the side of my

face. I could feel the texture of her skin and the pressure of her hand just as before. She often took my hand as it lay on the bed and held it in her own—but I couldn't grasp hers in response. An embodied pleasure I had actively enjoyed was holding Janet's hand when we walked together. I just wanted to touch her.

I often told myself, when doubtful of my "personhood," that if our positions were reversed and Janet had suffered catastrophic injury, I would still love her, still want to touch her, fuck her, still want to be her lover no matter what. And yet . . . I was so changed, and much more doubtful of my existential being than Janet seemed to be. "I am your physical lover, and I want to be your physical lover." Janet said that to me, exactly that, many times, but still . . .

So she climbed into bed with me, right there in room 120. She closed the door, walked around to the side of the bed, put down the rail, climbed in, and lay down behind me. I was positioned on my side, toward the chair she had been sitting in. She put her arm around me, her hand on my breast, and pressed her body along the length of mine. And there we lay. Because there was every chance of the door opening and someone walking in, we didn't fall asleep together, not because we were ashamed of being "caught," but because Janet didn't want to put the staff in an awkward position. We were both quite sure that getting into bed with a patient would be frowned upon, especially one catheterized and with a gastrointestinal tube. But she did stay pressed up against me for a while, and not a little while. When she got up, she came around to face me, and kissed me, and said, "I am your physical lover."

* * *

I've always loved fucking, ever since I discovered love and imperative desire. From tenth grade on, my group of friends and I had been harassed at Huntingdon Area Senior High School—we were "freaks" (in the lexicon of the late sixties). Most of the students were "straight." Some angry ones felt free to mock and laugh at us in the cafeteria. They made oinking noises when I walked past them in the hall, and shoved the boys against the lockers. As the parking lot emptied out, we'd hear threatening insults yelled from passing cars. I don't have a clear recollection of the decisive moment when my parents came up with the solution of enrolling me as a first-year student at Juniata, skipping my senior year of high school. While attending Juniata, I could apply elsewhere for acceptance as a transfer student. So the summer before my first year of college, I dropped away from my high school friends to hang out in the company of the woman who became my lover, one of a small group of left-wing, activist intellectuals at Juniata, a few of whom were spending the summer in Huntington before their senior year. How I idealized them! I wanted to be like them. I wanted to be with them.

As it happened, I simply wanted one woman in particular. As summer turned into fall, I started keeping a journal. Despite my friendships, I felt alone in the world, a wearing kind of existential loneliness (I was studying existentialism, so I knew, and I was seventeen years old, so I *really* knew). Many of the entries were about loneliness, a word I repeated so frequently on the pages of the yellow legal pad that the record is suffused with a sort of pathos, especially because I misspelled the word throughout. Sometime in the middle of the winter, I remember writing, "I wonder if I'm a lesbian," not a thought that had ever crossed my mind before. My desire to be in Kathy's company, however, was so insistent that the idea came unbidden.

I forget how it came about, but I went with Kathy to her parents' home in Delaware for a weekend visit. We stayed in her bedroom and slept together in a double bed. I felt Kathy's arm twitch as we lay together there, and, thinking she was in distress, reached out to stroke her face. As it happens, she was fine. Her body was moving as sleep overtook her, as I now know bodies do, but then my ignorance abetted my desire. She woke and turned to me, and we spent the night touching and talking and kissing—all pretty chaste, but quite hot enough. I knew I was in love and that I wanted more. I was reaching toward sexual pleasures that I couldn't then conceptualize, but that I fiercely desired, nonetheless. This was the time of free love, so the fact that she had a boyfriend, and that he lived just down the hall from me (in the "students' room" my parents rented out), seemed not to matter. She had never had a woman lover. I had had no lover at all. None of that was of any consequence—she had an apartment that she rented with another woman, and a mattress on the floor, and that was enough. All that mattered was kissing and touching, soon more adventuresomely, then lustfully, and the intimacy of private conversation.

I discovered that I liked sex a lot, and the particular closeness that it created for me. I was unashamed that I liked sex with women, and over the next eight years had lots of lovers, in the messy configurations of young lesbian-feminist communities professing non-monogamy, wherein women crossed often, if not often easily, from friendship to sexual partner, and back again to friendship. In those years, I was the one on the move, acting on my desires. Sex offered a kind of instant intimacy that I found both exciting and comforting, and the irresistible, invaluable sense that someone wanted me.

Sex ensured that I was not alone, but as my lover and I slowly passed into day-to-day routine, I'd get interested in someone else. I apparently couldn't bear intimacy as it crossed over into the regular patterns of an established relationship. I found that I was the one with a roving eye, and unsettled desires, the one leaving, rather than being left. I most likely still couldn't spell loneliness—but I didn't need to. It's only at a great distance from my younger self that I can see patterns emerging that would trouble my adult life, most notably my desire for intimacy contradicted by my (unconscious) fears that familiarity would inevitably morph into something familial. Only after long, sometimes strenuous, often difficult, and certainly belated learning have I been able to integrate my love of sex with intimacy over time.

* * *

In Janet, I have a lover who was more than willing to make sex happen even when we were separated by 2,579 miles, as we were at the first. She stopped to leave a message on her way to class at the University of Arizona. "You know, you're like St. Christina the Astonishing. I read about her last night. She's a twelfth-century Belgian whose miraculous breasts saved her when she was hiding from her persecutors in the wilderness—she was a virgin—she was starving—and her breasts gave her milk. Some say olive oil. Astonishing, but she's got nothing on you, baby. I'll call you again when I get home, sometime around 7:00 your time." She was on a pay phone next to the place she had just gotten a smoothie. (She was teaching Caroline Walker Bynum's book *Holy Feast and Holy Fast: The Religious Significance of Food to Medieval Women*.) That evening, I learned that phone-fucking with Janet was hot enough to make me hyperventilate. I've long known that my nipples are large and wonderfully sensitive, but it was Janet who discovered their true glory. She made me ecstatic.

My whole lifetime, I had moved through the world with my body, feeling my way, often with great pleasure and always by touch. With Janet, words came unbidden—my desires and my fears, and my hopes and my promises—until talking and fucking were wholly intertwined. With her I remain even now far as far can be from the ascetic Saint Christina, who longed to leave behind her husk of a body to be with God—I'm no saint, but when it comes to nipples, I am most certainly Christina the Astonishing. Breaking my neck destroyed countless neural pathways, but the damage to my body accelerates *below* my breastbone. I may not be able to sit up without secure support or turn over in bed, but my beautiful and astonishing nipples still can without difficulty stand erect as ever.

Over six years of loving Janet, I had learned a new way of "projecting before [myself] a sexual world," in the words of the philosopher Maurice Merleau-Ponty.[2] I learned the joy of sex. That is now a hackneyed phrase, but it concisely names a truth about our sexual life. Dialogue heightened sexual pleasure and created a deep knowing. Words matter. I'm so glad we talked as we did those six years we were lovers before the accident. In his study of "the phenomenology of perception," Merleau-Ponty argues that for humans, being is "a perpetual incarnation." You become who you are over the course of a life that unfolds as an ongoing interaction with objects and others, from the infant you once were, whose bodily cartography slowly emerged as you were handled by caregivers whose speech washed over you, to the grown-up you are today, drawn beyond reason to one person rather than another. Sexuality is elemental and irreducible, Merleau-Ponty argues, for sexual desire resists knowing and exceeds explanation. It's impossible to separate mind and body, sense and sensation, words and things. Merleau-Ponty also declares sex "ambiguous" because you can neither avoid it nor fully comprehend its imperatives. The etymology of the word in the *Oxford English Dictionary* is revealing—"Latin *ambigu-us* doubtful, driving hither and thither (< *ambig-ĕre*, < *amb-* both ways + *ag-ĕre* to drive) + OUS."[3] You're driven you know neither wither nor why, for sexuality is beyond interpretation.

There is no explanation of sexuality which reduces it to anything other than itself, for it is already something other than itself, and indeed, if we like, our whole being. Sexuality, it is said, is dramatic because we commit our whole personal life to it. But just why do we do this? Why is our body, for us, the mirror of our being, unless because it is a *natural self,* a current of given existence, with the result that we never know whether the forces which bear us on are its or ours—or with the result rather that they are never entirely either its or ours. There is no outstripping of sexuality any more than there is any sexuality enclosed within itself. No one is saved and no one is totally lost.[4]

My "current of given existence" had taken me to Janet's embrace. After she fucked me, I would lie full-length on top of her, while she held me on her chest and I talked to her. I spoke out of myself, as it were, saying into the darkness fears and desires too fugitive to mention in broad daylight. Fucking was sometimes sublime, and sex was a deep grappling with the human beings we each were, and the beings we were becoming through our sexual and spoken intercourse. It also was great fun. I swore to Janet that I loved every hair on her body—so much hair that it makes tufts at the bends of her knees and under her arms—a profuse surplus. So, in becoming sexualized subjects through our touch and talking, Janet and I lived into an unknown future.

*　*　*

October 1, 2003, began a new life. Thankfully, my desire for Janet is in no way incapacitated. This is not to say that I can get what I want. The spirit is very willing, but the body very weak. I'm her physical lover, as she is mine. I want her desire, and I have it. What I don't have is her touch. Or rather, my brain registers her touch as a pressure, but my body nonetheless remains out of reach. Not because Janet is unwilling to touch me, or because I shy away from touching her—to the contrary—but my *body can't know* how that touch feels. It's true that the brain is your most important sex organ, but the rest of the body needs to come online when called. Any part of me once innervated from C 5–6 down is now royally fucked up. I have become untouchable.

"It's like she's a stone butch," Janet said to her physician, resorting to simile in an effort to explain how things are. To any woman "in the life," a stone butch lesbian is a recognizable figure, like Jess in Leslie Feinberg's much-read novel—she's a woman who has cultivated "female masculinity" (Judith Halberstam's helpful phrase) to show herself as strong and capable of sheltering another woman and satisfying her desire, and sometimes to protect herself from feeling vulnerable.[5] A femme lesbian understands that her sexual responsiveness to the moves of her partner is what the stone butch desires—the butch woman may not wish to be sexually touched in return, or may wish it but find the prospect too overwhelming. When Janet used the simile "Christina's like a stone butch," she told the literal truth by way of metaphor. "Literal" means true "to the letter." I literally *can't* be touched, because my c-e-n-t-r-a-l n-e-r-v-o-u-s s-y-s-t-e-m i-s i-n-j-u-r-e-d, and it's a fucking tragedy.

When teaching students about figurative language, I tell them that "meta-" is a prefix denoting change (of place, order, condition, or nature), while "phor" is derived from an ancient Greek verb, "to carry" or "to bear." We can see metaphor as a condensed analogy, with the "phor" carrying an attribute out of its proper place to a different domain where it's improper, impertinent, out of place, and transformative. In Janet's simile, "stone butch" is "carried" from the world of lesbian bar culture to denote something about my life with her. By calling me "stone," Janet metaphorically represented my body's neurological incapacity as a sexual subject-position (stone butch). That's a catachresis—a strained metaphor—and bitter irony, considering that I *would love to be fucking differently with Janet, if I could.* "I've never been stone, *ever*! I've always wanted to touch *and* be touched," I protested. I nonetheless understood what she was trying to do, and why she would resort to metaphor. Neurological destruction has dealt a phenomenological blow that radiates beyond my body and creates epistemological conundrums that require troping. No wonder Janet reaches for metaphor in order to illuminate an embodied life that's opaque to both of us, and to cast light upon dark truths that require indirection. Thankfully, language is a renewable resource. So is sex, which—thank the stars above—we both continue to desire.

The brilliant writer Angela Carter conjures a sexual world of a "thousand and one Baroque intersections of flesh upon flesh" in her collection of perversely refigured fairytales, *The Bloody Chamber*. In so doing, she silently quotes the title of a collection of ancient and medieval stories from the Middle East, Persia, and South Asia, *A Thousand and One Nights*, also known as *The Arabian Nights*.[6] All those stories share the same framing device. A king marries a virgin, beds her, and preemptively executes her the next morning, before she has the chance to be unfaithful. Scheherazade avoids this fate by beginning on the wedding night to tell him a story, but leaving off before the end of her narrative. The king's curiosity to know what happens spares her, so the next night she does the same, and lives on to tell another, and another . . . so Scheherazade lives on and the king's desire remains lively. If sex is like language, so is language like sex. Each has a structuring system (grammar, the body) and a seeming infinity of possible statements one can make (sentences, sex acts). Both are most alive when energized by the speaking subject. Both have their reference books and guides to good usage. Most importantly for me, sex and language are both alive and enlivening, and link the life I've lived already to the living that opens before me. I need access to what once was, if I am to brave what is to come.

13

*

Supply
and Demand

"And how do you think all these things that you want are going to get done?" Janet said sharply. "Just tell me how they're going to get done." She was wheeling me through the living room one evening not long after I'd been discharged from the hospital, and we were fighting. A week before, a huge backhoe had made a big, muddy hole of our backyard, uprooting recently planted flower beds in the process. Just that afternoon, an enormous cement truck had (astonishingly) backed up into our driveway and had poured the cement for the foundation of the addition we were building so as to accommodate my paralyzed life. This was no longer the house we had bought, nor the yard we had enjoyed. I was not myself, and we were not leading the life we had envisioned. "I don't know," I said. "I just want it. I want it."

At that moment, I wanted the window shade in the front window of the living room to be straightened, because it bugged me when the shades weren't evenly positioned. I wanted to know if the mechanism was in some way damaged. I wanted it to be fixed. The misalignment didn't bother Janet, she may not even have noticed it, but now I was asking her to add the shade to the endless and ever growing to-do list that she carried around in her head. I was demanding her labor, and

I was driving her crazy, as she was making patently clear. Yet all the fight went out of her when I said, "I want it," without any further justification. Janet loved me for my ardent desires and my direct action, including my work of homemaking. I wanted to be able to keep the household as I had been doing before I was hurt—and I couldn't, an enormous loss for me. She knew as well as I did how accustomed I was to acting on my desires.

* * *

I did the fix-it jobs. I figured out how to make things work. I loved using my father's tools, all of which came to me. When Dad died, Jeff's paralysis had long since undone his grip, and, besides, he had his own (now unused) table saw in the basement, and his own (unused) toolbox. When we moved into our house with its quasi-finished basement, I bought a big piece of pegboard and hung everything up:

two sets of box wrenches, metric and imperial
two sets of combination wrenches, metric and imperial
two sets of hex keys
a monkey wrench
a set of slot screwdrivers
a set of Phillips head screwdrivers
a claw hammer
a ball-peen hammer
a rubber mallet
three vice grips, large, medium, and small

The socket wrenches (metric and imperial), spark plug wrench, ratchets, adjustable wrench, pipe wrench, drills, bits, wire cutter, wire stripper, and all the rest I had in a big red toolbox, and I arranged the hardware on shelves—task light and extension cord, screws, nuts and bolts, brackets, hooks, replacement doorknobs, and suchlike. I can see the tools clearly even now, arranged before me in memory.

I have a certain stubbornness that served me well when I was working on a job. When we moved into our house, we counted thirty-two windows, so we bought thirty-two window shades. Each had to be mounted. I started on the job when Janet was away, planning to finish it before she returned. Three windows later, I was frustrated by an angry blister starting on my palm, so, remembering my father's adage "the right tool for the right job," I went to the hardware store and bought an electric screwdriver. Later that day, much later, I stood back and observed my handiwork with Janet. "Wow—you did all that! Look how great that color is up against the paint we chose," she said admiringly, kissing me. "You're so butch and I'm so lucky."

These days we have a lovely yellow DeWalt cordless drill with power to spare and a full set of standard and screw-driving bits, though it came into our household too late for me. It is a gift from Colin, who works as an engineer at Black & Decker, the company that makes DeWalt tools. They're considered among the best—our contractor has exactly the same drill. When Colin mentioned that he was working on cordless drills, we developed a running joke about cordless drills and lesbian home life—no, not a sex joke, but rather a commentary on how household tasks are divvied up. Colin was game, even though joking happily about lesbians was new to him. We asserted that every proper lesbian household needs a cordless drill, and we were looking to him as a Black & Decker man to design a good one. It took him a while to "get" the joke, because it plays on the butchiness required of women living without men—somebody has to do the man's work. Or perhaps "All jobs are butch jobs." So says my high femme friend Lisa. The fabulous irony of this statement and its equally fabulous hyperbole are illegible unless you stop to reflect on butch-femme life. Lesbian households are not oppressed with a self-evident cultural norm that distributes beforehand domestic tasks into two and only two parts, the masculine ones and those left to the feminine side of the household. I know of a father so taken aback when his daughter told him she was in a lesbian relationship that he asked seriously, though supposedly in jest, "But who's going to mow the lawn?" Well, Dad, whoever is more butch, and since in lesbian bar culture what makes a good butch is her desire to please a femme, why not make all jobs butch jobs? That's Lisa's point.

As it happens, Janet is a butch-y femme and I'm a femme-y butch. She carries her wallet in the back pocket of her jeans and is comfortable in short skirts and four-inch heels. I've many times been told the women's restroom is no place for a man (me), yet I have many earrings and scarves, but no suits and ties. Gender is thus no sure guide of our division of labor. Before a spinal cord injury disabled me, any job requiring strength, from opening a jar to heaving around the rocks to build a patio, was mine. I crawled under the car and used duct tape to temporarily fix the VW's bumper when it got caught on something, pulled away from the frame of the car, and needed to be secured. I mounted the carrier for the kayaks on the roof of our car, and the bicycle carrier on the back. I always drove the motorcycle. I paid my bills and kept track of my money. I also enjoyed cooking and prepared all our meals, while Janet sat at the kitchen table and read to me. I shopped for groceries and almost always set the dining room table. I had a small KitchenAid mixer that had been decommissioned in the late 1950s from the Juniata College Home Economics Department, which allowed me to beat egg whites until they formed a stiff peak, before carefully folding them into sweetcorn stripped from cob. The result? Deliciously light corn fritters made by dropping the batter onto a hot griddle, as I had seen Mother make them. I also baked bread, made a light, flaky pie crust, and enjoyed cooking supper in the evening when Janet and I were together. I sewed on buttons, and did repair jobs on my clothing using a decommissioned sewing machine that came to me as the mixer had done, from the Home Ec. Department.

I did those jobs because I valued what the work produced. When Janet and I started living together, I figured that we would divide the work evenly, fifty-fifty, but it turned out that I care more about homemaking then she does, and set a higher value on it. I liked sitting down to good food and a glass of wine at a candlelit table, even for an ordinary supper, and I fully appreciated Janet's cleaning up afterward. Since she actually enjoyed doing the laundry, that job was hers, and I had folded underwear in my drawer for the first time in my life. We figured out that I liked having the surfaces in the living room clear, so she corralled papers that otherwise would have been strewn about. When I vacuumed her study, I would close the closet door—until I noticed that it was invariably open, so I asked if she preferred it that way. Remarkably, even incomprehensibly to me, the answer was yes. So I left it open, and would run the vacuum around piles of books on the floor. It took us about three years, but we had actually worked out a way to live together, intimately, in domestic space, with expectations and actions that mostly yielded happiness. If drifts of dog hair bothered me as they gathered in the corners, well, I could sweep them up while talking on the phone. If I noticed the shades were uneven and it bugged me, I could straighten them out. If I valued something more, noticed it more than Janet, why should I expect her to do the work? And vice versa. Of course there was friction. It's not that we didn't irritate or disappoint each other, but that such feelings were overbalanced by daily happiness and satisfaction, and leavened by unexpected delights.

* * *

How did we achieve such felicity? By fighting. I've learned that announcing forthrightly *that* you are angry *when* you are angry is the only way to love and happiness. The poet William Blake shows how it works.

A Poison Tree

I was angry with my friend;
I told my wrath, my wrath did end.
I was angry with my foe:
I told it not, my wrath did grow.

And I waterd it in fears,
Night & morning with my tears:
And I sunned it with smiles,
And with soft deceitful wiles.

And it grew both day and night,
Till it bore an apple bright.
And my foe beheld it shine,
And he knew that it was mine.

And into my garden stole,
When the night had veiled the pole;
In the morning glad I see;
My foe outstretched beneath the tree.[1]

I find it very difficult to directly announce my anger. Not that I'm not angry—far from it—but I fear the upset anger brings, and the almost certain fact that my anger will be repaid in kind. Harboring a grievance, however, is as fatal to happiness as Blake's poem suggests. When I'm angry with Janet, of course I see her as a foe. Yet because of who I am, I find it easier to deflect my anger than to forthrightly declare myself annoyed or put out by some "little" thing, and that's the perfect opening to deceit. The speaker of the poem may announce that he's glad his foe lies dead, but we know better. Anger is fertile ground, and the apple of discord destroys delight. Surely this is true in the narrative of the poem, where the plot replicates the original Fall from Paradise, thrusting you ever further into discord and darkness.

I think I'll always remember one of the first fights Janet and I had soon after we were living in the same house. I have no memory of what we were fighting about, but I do know that I couldn't stand it and walked away—I went upstairs to lie down on the bed. Subsequently, Janet appeared at the head of the stairs, asking, "What do you want?" The fight was still on, she was not solicitous, but rather pursuing the disagreement. I continued silent, and discovered that formulating what I wanted wasn't easy. I doubt I knew what I wanted clearly enough to compose a sentence. Or perhaps I knew, but it seemed unreasonable, not a demand—or even a request or observation—that I could in good conscience make. No matter. The point is to tell your wrath so that it might end. You may laugh when I say that it's turtles all the way down, but it's true. You'd better have some way of representing what you think and feel, for your thinking and feeling are already representing the world to you. You must know what you want to get it. We worked hard on our fighting, because we figured out that neither one of us wanted conflict to be destructive. We both wanted to be capable of fighting productively. Conflict can only be truly over and done when there's a negotiated outcome all parties find acceptable.

* * *

Then came my accident and the crash of our home economy. If I were to satisfy my needs by turning to Janet, let alone my wants, I would run up a truly unsustainable, bankrupting debt. Spinal cord injury is imperious, and we had no choice but to accept what I believe will be an interminable regime of austerity. Janet told me, very truly and not in wrath, but with a terrible finality, "You can't have what you want. You just can't." There's no way that she can respond to every wish of mine for this or for that—even if she has the skill, she may not have the inclination, and she certainly doesn't have the time. And since one day leads into another, the demand is never ending.

Perfect equilibrium of value is supposedly achieved in an imaginary economy when the supply curve (the goods offered by producers) meets precisely with the demand curve (consumer desire) for those commodities. In our case, we pay many, many thousands of dollars a year to those who help meet our needs and desires: an aide who helps with my personal care (twenty hours per week), another on weekends (sixteen hours per month), and workers who clean the house, deliver groceries, rake leaves, shovel snow, and walk the dog midday in the city (because I can't pick up her poop)—all because I'm paralyzed. We buy the commodity these workers have for sale, so many hours of their labor power, because we can no longer do the work ourselves. There's a broken lamp shade in our living room that I "repaired" with packing tape months ago. It's been hanging askew ever since. I thought I could actually fix this problem by ordering another shade off the web, but the fitting of the lamp needs to be altered. The demand for labor far exceeds what we can supply in-house, and buying labor power is limited both by our ability to pay and what the job market offers. We have terrific helpers of all sorts,

I can't imagine better, yet we still haven't found a skilled handyman, and not for want of trying. Moreover, purchasing the help we need is complicated by the intimacy of many of the jobs that need doing. After all, these workers are in our home for hours every day, supporting our supposedly private lives.

Janet and I have largely recovered our equilibrium. She does so much to aid my "activities of daily living" that surely I can see a cockeyed lamp or window shade in the living room without distress. I can wait patiently while she does household tasks that I used to do. I can learn not to want. Yet at the same time, I know that my visceral wanting was, in part, what attracted Janet to me. She was drawn to my desire for daily pleasures and my readiness to act so as to realize that desire, so not-wanting is hardly what I want to do. I must do just that, nonetheless, if we are to live sustainably. We are unspeakably fortunate. We both have good, secure jobs, and a joint income that frees us from the nagging daily worry about money that is so enervating. In a world where so many live truly precarious lives, I would be a fool not to value what I have, and realize the real abundance I enjoy with Janet. I'm no fool. But I won't say it's easy.

14

❉

Shameless Hussy,
Babe D., Moxie Doxie

Shameless Hussy came to me as airline freight I received at the airport that serves Providence, Rhode Island. I was twenty-two, starting graduate school without support from Brown University, using money I had earned the year before, my first out of college. I didn't have a car, and had only been in Providence three weeks, but I found an acquaintance who drove me out and back. It didn't take long to collect the animal-shipping crate that was waiting for me and return to Elmwood, a once grand but now poor neighborhood. I got dropped off in front of the three-story house where I rented a two-room apartment, learned to live with cockroaches, and shared the bathroom down the hall with the man who lived across from me. The place was about two miles across the city from Brown, over the dividing line of the interstate. I carried my burden up the three flights to my two rooms. When at last I opened the crate, a little bundle of rust-colored fur stepped out, having lived but eight weeks in the world, squatted, peed on the linoleum floor, and we began our life together.

Her tail had no hair in the middle, just a tuft at the end, so she looked like a little lion—she was the runt, and the other puppies had gnawed off everything but that little bit. She was the only one of the litter left when Teresa (my lover from Swarthmore days) drove out of D.C. to McLean, Virginia, to get her. Teresa knew I wanted a mixed-breed retriever, having lost my heart to one on a cold winter day in Rock Creek Park, and she had followed with me the classified ads in the *Washington Post* for months. I wanted to have the warmer weather for housebreaking my puppy and begin obedience training before I had to leave to start graduate school. "You know I can't get one now," I said when she called me in mid-September about the ad for Irish setter–golden retriever puppies, $25 each. "I don't know anyone around here who could take her out when I have to go to school! I live on the third floor, and I'm absolutely broke—I can't pay anyone to help me. I only have a bicycle to get to school and back . . . How the hell am I going to housebreak a puppy?" I knew perfectly well that I couldn't get a dog, and three days later called to say, "See if there's one left." Now I had a little creature with burnished red hair, floppy ears, and a lion's tail. She needed a name.

Standing in the stacks of the John D. Rockefeller, Jr. Library as I searched for books on John Dryden for my course on eighteenth-century British literature, I suddenly thought "Shameless Hussy." It is the name of a small feminist press that was one of the very first. I clearly needed a powerful antidote to the concatenation of wealthy, white, patriarchal social, cultural, and economic power that was the Rock, as the library is called. Brown was named to honor the family who over the eighteenth century dedicated themselves to building the institution. They were rich merchants who participated in the slave trade, as did many in Providence—60% of the slave ships that were part of the North American triangle trade sailed from its port, some years more than 90%. Brown was perforce enriched by donations and bequests of wealth amassed in that lucrative trade. As for the university library, it was named to honor its wealthy benefactor. A Brown graduate, Rockefeller Jr. became in his later years known for his philanthropy—but he also infamously owned a controlling interest in the Colorado Fuel and Iron Company when it was responsible for the 1914 Ludlow massacre, the torching of a tent camp of striking workers that killed twenty, mostly women and children. I understood perfectly well that no university is endowed with "clean money," because there's none in the world to be had. I was having a hard time anyway. I needed to imaginatively distance myself from the institution of which I was now a part, if I were to have any hope of succeeding there. I had left behind a flourishing lesbian-feminist community in D.C. Teresa worked at First Names First, a feminist bookstore the very title of which protests patriarchal naming traditions—*she* would approve of Shameless Hussy's name, for sure. What better than an uncontrollable, powerful, sexed-up virago to keep me connected to my lover and the community I had just left?

I had the great advantage of having gotten, simply by chance, a puppy who was disposed to please me. As for myself, I was alone and lonely, and glad of her company. I couldn't study all the time, so Hussy and I went over the basic commands again and again. When it came time to train her off lead, we walked a block over to a big weedy graveyard that had a waist-high chain-link fence around it, where I lifted her over, then climbed over myself. It was a big graveyard, but completely fenced in—if she disobeyed me, she couldn't run away and get lost. I hid behind the gravestones when teaching her to stay, a lesson she learned very, very well. We were each other's sole companions for more than a month until I began making friends. Of course she destroyed things—she was a puppy! I had taped to the wall one of the only mementos I had of the world I had left behind, a photo of the softball team on which I had played catcher, and when it fell, she tore it up and doubtless ingested some of the pieces. Shameless Hussy also ate a rubber plant, the covers of my Virginia Woolf and Henry James paperbacks, and half of my Swarthmore diploma. I didn't mind much—she was good company, and by the second semester was old enough to run on the sidewalk alongside my bicycle, stopping at the curbs until I released her, waiting for me as I labored up College Hill, and then patiently lying by my bicycle as I did my work at Brown. Some days she ran the four-mile round-trip to Brown, and would go another four miles with me if I took a run in the evening, which I sometimes did. She was lean, muscular, and handsome, and people would stop me on the street to tell me so.

I had gotten admitted to the Ph.D. program of Brown University's Department of English, but since they offered me no support, I clearly hadn't been one of their first choices. There were a number of classmates in the same fix, who had decided to shelter in graduate school against a deep recession that made finding a job seem impossible, and we were all trying to prove our worth. Perhaps that underdog position bonded me even more with the little puppy who stepped out of the crate. She grew into a handsome and well-trained dog, and I turned out to be a stronger student than my initial position foretold. I was awarded the support of teaching assistantships after that first year, and when it came time to write my dissertation, I applied to Wellesley College for—and won—a year-long Alice Freeman Palmer grant established to support the higher education of women. The grant is "for study or research abroad or in the United States. The holder must be no more than twenty-six years of age at the time of her appointment and unmarried throughout the whole of her tenure." I knew that would not be a burdensome requirement, and was glad not only for the money, but for the connection to a nineteenth-century feminist. I wrote a dissertation. Carried on the great wave of "poststructuralism," I got a great job at Wesleyan as an assistant professor. Hussy saw me through the six years of work leading up to my successful review for promotion with tenure, which decided whether I would keep or lose my job. A year after that climactic event, she got sick. She had lived fifteen years, but now a tumor in her spleen was growing and unstoppable. "See here," the veterinarian said, gesturing to the sonogram, "you can see how it's pushing the organs out of place. But she's not in pain. She probably has two or three months, you'll just have to care for her as she gets weak." Oh God, nothing to do? Nothing at all? I cried hard for a long time in the car in the parking lot, petting Hussy as she lay quietly on the seat beside me, before I turned the key and drove home.

I chose her death when she was unable to eat. Sitting in the backseat of my car, I held her in my lap as the vet injected her with a fatal dose. She was my first dog, had been my wonderfully physical companion as I lived through the formative and deforming years of professionalization, and I grieved her loss. But I knew even at that terrible moment that I would have another dog.

* * *

"Is this the day?" Babe D. (a.k.a. Babe the Dog) asked every morning, "Is today the day?" Janet and I were sitting up in bed, where we ate cereal and drank tea every morning. Babe was on Janet's side of the bed, with her hind legs on the floor and her upper body on the duvet cover—that's all the farther she was allowed. She reached out and put her left paw on Janet's left leg. "No." She took it off. She put it back on. "No." Janet suffered this a few more times and then told her, "Off," and Babe learned that for yet another day, she didn't get to dominate Janet—she knew better then to ask me, because I was securely in the alpha position of our pack, while Janet was beta, and Babe invariably gamma. She nonetheless asked every day if, overnight, the order of things had changed. Babe D. was named in honor of Babe Didrikson, the best athlete of the twentieth century, and she lived up to that indomitable competitor's name.

I began looking in the classifieds about two years after Shameless Hussy's death, and after a couple of months, found what I was searching for—a litter of half white lab, half golden retriever puppies, $50 each. When I went to see them, I looked for the smallest one, as if to channel Shameless Hussy, paid my money, and started walking away with "Tiny," as the owner of the bitch called her, in my arms. But Babe, whom I first saw draped over the shoulders of one of the other puppies, decided I was the best thing going, and came running after me, with her little ears flapping. She was a real looker, mostly white, with a blush of color on the tips of her ears and the top of her head, while Tiny had no such advantages. So Babe went home with me.

For the first three years of her life, she was a hellion. She would look directly at me, our eyes would meet, and I could see her deciding whether she was going to obey my command. I had no convenient fenced-in field, so I was training her outside on a long lead. I named her so that I could yell in public, "Babe, come here!" Good thing, because we practiced the recall command over and over. When she was older and *almost* 100% reliable, I would sometimes forgo the leash, especially if I was in a hurry. Now and then, of course, when I called her to come, she'd turn around, and take off, with me in hot pursuit, sprinting through the backyards of my neighborhood and quickly calculating where I might corner her. Great fun for the dog, but when I finally tackled her and grabbed her by the scruff of the neck, she knew she was in disgrace. I guess the iconic moment was this: Before leaving for class one bright fall afternoon, I opened the door into the backyard for her, where she knew to relieve herself in amongst some ivy and scrub bushes. By then, I had had her for maybe two and a half years, and she was off lead while I waited for her by the door. She took off, I ran after. Going fast, she disappeared around a corner—and was gone. Damn! I was already late, and could only hope that she would head for campus one block over and not run down to the busy street one block below. Coming home I looked for her everywhere and kept calling her, with no luck. I was getting ready to go out on my bicycle to extend my search when a Wesleyan Public Safety cruiser pulled up. I could see Babe happily sitting on the front seat, panting, with her ears cocked, beside the uniformed officer, who stepped out and called, "Excuse me, ma'am, is this your dog?" He had checked the tag on her collar, which had my phone number and address, and had brought her home. "She was in the Science Center, got up to the second floor somehow. The students were pretty happy about it. Here she is," and he handed her over. So, escorted by a uniformed officer, she came home.

If you had told me then that she would become a well-trained dog, who would stay right beside me (off lead!) when we went out for an afternoon run, and always come when called, I would have laughed derisively. Yet she did turn into a well-behaved dog and one I loved unreservedly. I could even look at her puppy pictures without cursing. Home in the evening, I would take her out back for a game of "tennis ball" that sent her tearing down the hill. Back she would come with the ball in her mouth. Dropping it at my feet, she'd tell me to DO IT AGAIN. In bad weather, I'd sit inside at the top of the stairs and bounce her ball down. Down she would rush after it and back up she would come, two steps at a time, down and back, endlessly. Only hot and humid weather could tire her out. I'm sure that to anyone who didn't particularly like dogs, such routines would seem insufferably repetitious and boring, but I found her wholly engaging in her enthusiasm and simple happiness, and welcomed the familiarity of our play.

Janet enjoyed Babe's company, too, and, having trained a dog herself, understood quite clearly the question Babe posed every morning. We both found her amusing, and the three of us formed a unit with clearly articulated, harmonious relationships, insofar as any pack where species meet can so establish itself. In warmer weather, when we left the front door open, Babe would sit for hours looking out the bottom half of the storm door, now and again jumping up in great agitation. We knew what she was doing—she was watching squirrel TV, always the same channel, always the same program, always squirrels. When it got cold, I was sorry to turn off the TV by shutting the door. Babe also harbored a desire to meet skunks, as we discovered one evening when I let her go off lead to relieve herself behind the house. She returned in a minute or two, but as she approached, stopped to rub her muzzle against first one, then the other front leg. Something was bothering her. A nearer approach, and I knew what. As Janet imagines the scene, the dog saw a skunk and excitedly asked, "Can *I* smell *your* butt—*right now*? Can I, can I??" She got sprayed right between the eyes. I had heard that tomato juice countered skunk oil, so I opened every can of tomatoes and tomato juice in the cupboard, including Newman's Own Marinara Sauce, and dumped the contents over her while Janet went to the closest convenience store for more. She returned with bottles of Bloody Mary mix that I poured over the dog and tried to rub into her coat. She smelled like skunk for a long, long time—I can't recommend it as a treatment. She did not, thankfully, turn pink.

* * *

Fortunately for the three of us, "Can I smell your butt?" became for Janet and me an oft-repeated phrase announcing our dog's enthusiastic approach to the world. Babe was always puppy-like in her hopefulness, and had never really grown into the big feet that had promised a larger dog, so she looked puppy-like, too. One year Janet was living in Cambridge, and when I went to visit, we often walked with Babe to a noodle shop just off Harvard Square. I looped her leash to a chair outside, and she sat there waiting for us to carry out our food and join her. We watched her through the big front widows as she repeatedly beguiled passersby, who stopped to talk with her and scratch her behind the ears—the most popular dog in Cambridge, Janet and I observed in justified hyperbole. It's the making of such accounts that enriched our social unit, giving my relation to Janet and hers to me greater depth and complexity, because we weren't alone—we had Babe in our lives. Here I want to be vividly clear. We did NOT think of Babe as a child, so please don't get confused by my effort to narrate the pleasures of living in the social unit of a pack. I was never Babe's mother, I have no floppy ears. No, our pack had two human beings and one dog being, and was a formation in which Babe the Dog, Janet, and I made a domestic life together. Babe enhanced our social world, made runs more fun and walks more adventuresome, turned raking leaves into a game, did the same by dropping her ball in front of the lawnmower, and by plunging into any available body of water, including a little stream that ran through a wooded ravine not far away. When she'd come splashing out, her undercarriage would be black with mud. I had to hose her off, no big deal.

One night I woke up to the sound of Babe falling down the stairs. It took me a moment to figure out what was going on, and when I got down to the living room, she was wobbling about dazed. Janet was in NYC. I got Babe to lie down, and lay down on the floor alongside her, telling her over and over that she was a good dog. After a while, we both went to sleep. I woke up stiff, and she had a lump on her head from her tumble down the stairs, but was otherwise her indefatigable, enthusiastic self. Whatever had happened remained unexplained. One evening a few years later, she was suddenly having a seizure, right there in the kitchen with Janet and me. Our veterinarian's answering service referred us to an emergency clinic in West Hartford—Janet drove while I held Babe in my lap, stroking her and whispering in her ear as her body trembled and jerked. And then, just like that, the seizure stopped. When we got out of the car fifteen minutes later, she jumped out wagging her tail, ears up, completely her sociable self. *I'm* glad to see *You*, Babe informed both the veterinarian and her assistant. Are *You* glad to see *Me*? We learned that there was nothing we could do, other than be thankful that the seizure was over with no apparent damage. The next time, though, everything was different.

* * *

I had been home from the hospital for six or seven months, and had gone out with Babe to let her relieve herself behind the garage. I was wheeling myself slowly up the path to the deck, when she ran past on the lawn and jumped to get up where the deck was lowest. There was a pipe that she didn't see, and she hit her head *hard* just above her eyes. She immediately went into convulsions, neural circuits in her brain flooded with incapacitating voltage, and began staggering spastically around the yard with her tongue out and her eyes rolling back in her head.

I looked on aghast, and turned to go back down the path hoping I could somehow reach her. HELP HELP HELP WOULD SOMEBODY PLEASE HELP ME HELP HELP! In turning the wheelchair, I had wedged it between the stone walls along the path (my turning radius was too large, as I now know), and was hopelessly stuck. The more I struggled, the clearer it became that I couldn't help her—I couldn't even help myself. Oh God Oh God HELP PLEASE PLEASE HELP I NEED HELP MY DOG AND I NEED HELP . . . finally I saw a woman come running around the side of my neighbor's house with her maybe ten-year-old son. She dislodged my wheelchair and helped me into the house, then went back outside where the boy had remained with Babe. I fumbled to find the phone number for our veterinarian, utterly frantic, and at last was able to dial. "Somebody is coming, we will send somebody out, she's on her way, she really is, she's coming." She did come. By then Babe was no longer actively seizing, and had been carried into the house by my neighbors. The veterinarian's assistant injected her with a medication that should—and did—ensure she would stay quiet. Thank you, thank you, I said to everyone, thank you.

Then I was alone with Babe. I couldn't lie down next to her, could only lean down to touch her where she lay quietly on her bed, and even that was hard to do because I had to heave myself back up into a sitting position and I wasn't very strong. Worse—I knew I couldn't really comfort her, because she could not get used to the wheelchair, which means she was a shade uncomfortable with me. The chair made her uneasy, and no wonder—it's a big and cumbersome machine that moves around, stops, and moves around again. Our pack had been dispersed and her routine profoundly disrupted for half a year, and even though I was home from the hospital, I was far from the person she had known in the alpha position of our pack. I had so looked forward to seeing her again, and Janet, too, had been anticipating the reunion. Poor Babe. She recognized me, but kept her distance and didn't excitedly come over to greet me. It broke my heart. My relationship with her had been a fully embodied one. Dogs understand us as much by our posture and gestures as through words, and although she knew who I was, there was no recovering our old closeness. How I cried over the loss of that treasured, physical intimacy! How cruel of the fates to decree the alienation of her affection, by returning me to her so strangely altered.

The seizure when she hit her head was a prelude to seizures that began in earnest some months later. Every few days she had a seizure, and though none lasted longer than a few minutes, those were hard minutes to bear since there was nothing we could do. She was probably suffering a brain tumor, and there was nothing to be done but help her be calm after each neurological storm. On Christmas Day the three of us got into the van, and Janet drove over to the large cemetery covering much of Indian Hill, adjacent to the campus. The day was sharply cold, but sunny. Babe did fine walking and I was okay rolling the big loop around the graves. In fact, she was very much her enthusiastic self, forging ahead and looking back so that we would come on, already. Just after Christmas, we had to leave town for a few days. We were fortunate that her veterinarian worked in a practice that included a kennel where she always stayed when we left town, and the doctor made sure that the staff understood her vulnerability. They promised to watch over her carefully. The day we got back was too late to go get her, so the next morning Janet went out to pick her up first thing. Donna was helping me with my routine of care when Janet came back alone. "Babe is too sick to come home—the seizures became so frequent that they had to keep her heavily tranquilized. Doctor Brothers thinks her time has come. We need to go back together." We didn't talk about it for long, because there was no question about what we had to do. When the attendant brought her into the little examination room where we were waiting, I don't know that Babe could clearly distinguish who Janet was—although she staggered forward to where Janet was sitting on the floor. I could only reach down to touch Babe's head. There was a Medi-Port on her rear leg, where Doctor Brothers inserted a needle. Then we were left alone with our dead dog, who looked a lot younger than her twelve years—because she was white, there was no grizzled muzzle to indicate her age.

Recalling this event still hurts my heart, in part because my love for her was so physically thwarted after I got home from the hospital. At this mournful moment of her death, I couldn't join Janet in cradling her as Doctor Brothers ushered her out of the world. I could just barely run my hand down her back. I had already been grieving for the closeness with her that I lost when I returned from the hospital so terribly transformed—now my tears flowed into the finality of death.

*   *   *

Moxie Doxie is the name of the little white bichon frise now sleeping in my lap, the best hand warmer around, since dogs' temperatures run higher than ours. I consider her name truly inspired. So far, only my colleagues in early modern studies and one particularly sharp eighteenth-century scholar have understood the full significance of the rhyme. "Moxie," as you doubtless know, signifies "courage, audacity, spirit"—its etymology takes you back to nineteenth-century America, when Moxie was the name of an all-purpose fortifying tonic peddled door to door. The name of the potion came to signify as a metonym for the qualities necessary to hawk it. You had to have moxie to sell Moxie. As for "doxie" (or doxy, doxye), the *Oxford English Dictionary* tells you that the word was "[o]riginally the term in Vagabonds' Cant for the unmarried mistress of a beggar or rogue: a beggar's trull or wench: hence, slang, a mistress, paramour, prostitute; dial., a wench, sweetheart."[1] In short, a hussy—"a disreputable woman of improper behavior."[2] Shameless Hussy and Moxie Doxie are quite the same—as names. As dogs, they're not.

Moxie Doxie is not a retriever of any kind, though she does enjoy playing a round of "go get it" with a floppy, squeaky toy. She's a breed raised for centuries to be petted. Favored by royalty in sixteenth-century France, her "job" is to hang around with you and be charming, and so she is, thirteen and a half pounds of tightly curled white hair, with floppy ears that cock when she's listening, a short muzzle, black nose, and round, dark eyes—all very appealing. I need a dog that will come to me and climb up, since I can't lie down on the floor to play. I feared I would have retriever envy, but I don't—those days are over. Moxie's a happy dog who sometimes presents me with a toy to tug and throw, and who will amuse herself by violently shaking and tossing a toy to then run after. Her presence is welcome and comforting.

It's true that I can't be with her as with her predecessors—I can't play chase with her, running from room to room, or roll around with her on the floor, and I actively miss that play. I also can't be the kind of trainer that I was when working with Shameless Hussy and Babe. I can't assume the erect posture of the leader, can't swoop down on her when she's getting into trouble, and can't religiously enforce the recall command until she understands that she must come to me, no matter what. So she doesn't. Nonetheless, Janet and I together have managed to train her pretty well, though she'll never be as responsive to voice commands as I wish. I enjoy the other-mindedness of interacting with her, and the pleasures of just hanging around. I like being companionable with dogs, who like being companionable with us. Dogs are all body all the time and our sociability with them is largely an embodied affair. That's not to say there's no thinking. There is plenty of thinking on both her part and mine, and I communicate with her, chair and all. She's never known me otherwise, and I make a happily livable life with Janet and her in the ever repeated present of dog time.

15

✳

Anabaptist Reformations

"You're going to love this wedding," Jeff said to Janet and me. Kirsten and Matt's wedding was to be on the following day, and Jeff, in his excitement, wanted Janet and me to feel what he was feeling. This desire, a subtle and generous emotional coercion, was all too familiar to me, since Mother would quietly exert unspoken affective expectations to ensure familial harmony. Jeff, quite unconsciously, I think, very much wanted us to like what he liked, love what he loved, feel what he felt. To be part of his family. Weddings, however, were never going to be for me what they were for him. I am the lesbian of the family and a feminist, too. I have no interest whatsoever in getting married. To the contrary. Janet and I both hold the belief that "marriage enslaves all women," a radical feminist view from the 1970s that neither of us has seen any reason to abandon.

I am, of course, being deliberately provocative. It's simply true, however, that marriage is a contract enforced by the state that establishes the family as a private unit, within which women have always done the unremunerated work of reproduction, not only bearing children, but caring for them and their husbands, too. Gay marriage might have been an opportunity to rethink the institution, but I don't see that happening—I see instead the same focus on "personal responsibility" and private life. Childrearing is the nucleus of the nuclear family, whether parents are straight or gay, and that's been privatized, too, with the disappearance of subsidized, affordable day care and hollowing out of public education by private charter schools. This festival of normativity and so-called private life, and the narrative of "progress" that goes with it, suggests that there is no other way to organize sexual relations and social life than the nuclear family, no other way to love or to bring children into the world and help them grow up. I understand that for some couples, marriage is a sacrament, and that's fine with me. If you think that getting married in the eyes of God will celebrate your love, help you stay married, and help you rear children well, go ahead. But let religious institutions do the marrying, and *take the state out of it*. Let marriage become a commitment sealed in a religious ceremony, rather than a contract notarized by the state. No more trips to the courthouse for a license, and no more puritanical, punctilious horror of licentiousness. No pressure to get married in order to have access to the good things in life. Under those conditions, even I might learn to love a wedding.

* * *

Janet and I had driven to Lancaster to be with my family and to participate in this wedding, despite our reservations about the institution, and would sit in the front rows as a recognized couple among other members of the family. Now we were visiting with my dear brother as he lay in his hospital bed in the Moravian Manor. He didn't want to give us any information about exactly *what* we were going to like about the wedding, and the conversation quickly hurried along to many details—we were to meet up at the church at such and such a time, be seated in the front pews by the ushers, the reception would be held in an art gallery in downtown Lancaster that rented out its space for such events, we could park both his van and mine in the back lot . . . the caterer . . . the guests . . . the tuxedos. . . . He was excited, happy, talkative, and a bit anxious. The pictures of the wedding party show him sitting in his chair, handsome in a dark blue suit.

As it turned out, he was right—in a way. I *did* like what Kirsten and Matt had made of the wedding ceremony. In contrast to the outlandish elaborations created by the wedding industry and laid out in Kodachrome-color displays, their ceremony was simple and in important ways unexpected. Gerbera daisies, not orchids, were their flower of choice, and the flowers as they used them quietly undid conventional expectations of gender. As each bridesmaid came down the aisle, she held before her a daisy, which she gave to Matt, who was standing to the side of the chancel, waiting for the bride. When he saw Kirsten, attended by Beth, appear at the back of the sanctuary, he walked up the aisle and presented his bride with what had become a real handful of daisies. Matt—the groom!—walked the length of the aisle to the back of the church holding the flowers before him so as to give them to Kirsten, a transfer that transformed the daisies into the bride's traditional bouquet. These tweakings of the profoundly heteronormative ceremony of marriage mattered to me, as did other small changes. There was no effort to divide the congregation down the middle, for example, between people "belonging" to the bride and people "belonging" to the groom, and no "giving away" of the bride, all metaphors of property that I find absurd and offensive.

Once the bridesmaids were assembled behind the bride on one side of the chancel and the groomsmen lined up behind the groom on the other, however, the inventiveness of the processional evaporated. Kirsten stood before the congregation arrayed in a white satin, off-shoulder bridal gown with a vividly orange sash and a long, white satin train spread around her. Kirsten is a beautiful woman, and she looked simply gorgeous with her blonde hair swept up behind into a formal chignon, a style echoed by the bridesmaids. Their gowns were also strapless. Both the hairstyle and dress style Kirsten chose require saturation in femininity to look their best, which meant some of the party inevitably showed how hard they were trying. (By the time the reception rolled around, even Kirsten had tugged once or twice at the bodice. "A fatal error," Janet observed, drawing on her own experience, "because you simply have to trust in the structure of the gown and whatever tape you have surreptitiously introduced to keep it in place. Once you start tugging, it's all over.") Looking to the right of the chancel, I considered that groomsmen are, in general, truly out of luck, since I've never seen a rented tuxedo that actually *fits*, although Matt did fill his out quite handsomely. By now the whole event was resolving into "a wedding," and I thought, well, they tried.

Then Kirsten did something unexpected. She stepped behind the pulpit, came back to the middle of the chancel carrying a folding metal chair, opened it, and sat down. As she did so, Matt also turned to the side. He picked up a basin full of water, draped a towel over his arm, and then walked over and stood in front of Kirsten. She took off her white pumps. He put the basin in front of her and knelt down in his tuxedo to wash her feet. Then he dried them carefully, and she slipped her shoes back onto her feet. They changed places, with Kirsten kneeling in front of the basin, the satin of her gown and train spread all around her. Matt took off his lustrous black wingtips and his socks, and Kirsten gently washed and dried his feet. He had a bit of a struggle pulling his dress socks over his damp feet, but managed to get his shoes on before the organist's music ended. Matt put away the chair and Kirsten put away the basin and towel. The service then unfolded in a more conventional way.

This foot-washing ritual is familiar to all baptized Brethren, but I had never before seen or heard of it being incorporated into a wedding ceremony. By including foot washing, the bride and groom testified to their belief in the theological radicalism of the Brethren faith: that military service contravenes the will of God, that we are called to humility, simplicity, and service to others, that one who is rich in spirit is poor in nothing, and that we are called to share the Good News of salvation and reunion with God. Foot washing is the first act performed when a Brethren congregation assembles for Love Feast and Communion, in remembrance of the Passover meal the Gospels tell us that Jesus shared with his disciples on the eve of His crucifixion and resurrection. Before breaking bread, He knelt before His followers to wash the dust from their feet, and Kirsten and Matt reenacted this gesture of humility and service. In the Brethren tradition of my youth, however, there was a crucial difference in the ceremony—the congregation was segregated by gender, as you will soon see. I doubt that Kirsten and Matt intended a critical commentary on Brethren gender when they wrote foot washing into their wedding ceremony, but it's the part of their event that I liked the best.

* * *

I remember particular scenes of my time living in the Mission House quite vividly, as most children have distinct, if isolated, memories of their young lives. One is hanging upside down by my knees on a lower limb of a maple tree growing by the side of the house, showing off for Mother, who smilingly looked at me from a window. Another is of waiting for Mother and Dad to return home from church in the evening, where they had gone to celebrate the service of Love Feast and Communion. The service began with the men and the women dividing, each group going its separate way for the ceremony of foot washing. The sexes reconvene afterward for the ceremony of Communion, when purple grape juice in small Communion glasses and pieces of unleavened bread in a basket covered with a white napkin are passed around the table, followed by a simple meal invoking the last supper the disciples reportedly shared with Christ.

As a child, I knew firsthand about the grape juice and unleavened bread, because the Communion ceremony was held twice yearly in the sanctuary as part of a regular Sunday's service. But I wasn't yet allowed to take Communion. I couldn't participate until I was baptized, and that wouldn't happen for years, not until I was thirteen. So the breadbasket and the clinking tray of Communion glasses filled with grape juice passed me by. When Mother and Dad went to the evening service, it was a different matter, because I knew they would bring home one or two of the leftover ham salad sandwiches, food that had been prepared for the Love Feast by one of the Sunday school classes for grown-ups. These leftovers were a special treat for Jeff and me. I can still conjure up the particular flavor of that ham salad, though I haven't tasted it for more than forty years.

By the time I was thirteen, and enrolled in the class taught by our pastor to prepare us for baptism, I was beginning to feel that I was playing a part expected of me, and rather resented this extra obligation on top of Sunday school and worship every Sunday. I nonetheless went, sometimes wondering at my own disengagement from the upcoming ceremony at the heart of the Anabaptist tradition, "adult" baptism. I didn't feel much like an adult, though I did feel special on that day I joined other girls my age in a Sunday school classroom where we put on our bathing suits, and then pulled on simple white cotton gowns. We lined up and went barefoot down a plastic runway that had been laid over the linoleum floor of the hallway, onto the dark red rug of the sanctuary, up the stairs of the chancel, right to the edge of a large tank filled with water. It was revealed, flush with the floor where it had always been, unseen. When not being used to baptize believers, it was empty beneath the chancel table and hidden underneath the rug. Four steps down, and I was waist high with my gown floating around me, facing the pastor who stood there in his thoroughly soaked white robe. I knelt, which brought my chin to water level. He put one hand under my chin and the other on the top of my head, and dunked my head under three times, "In the name of the Father—the Son—and the Holy Ghost." I stepped out soaked and dripping, baptized into the Church of the Brethren.

Admitted to the celebration of Love Feast and Communion on the verge of puberty, I found myself increasingly ill at ease, out of place, unhappy. But mostly I felt trapped, a feeling rendered more emphatic by virtue of segregation by gender, for I had to follow Mother. The congregation assembled in the Fellowship Hall, a large, linoleum-floored room in the basement of the church with a big kitchen adjacent and a small stage at one end. Long folding tables were covered with tablecloths and place settings, and fluorescent lights shone overhead. After the invocation and a hymn, the women and girls went into an adjacent room, leaving the men and boys . . . where? Perhaps in the Fellowship Hall. No matter—it was the ominous, unimaginative, unfair, and increasingly ubiquitous separation of girls from boys that oppressed me. I had my prayer covering pinned on, a small net cap like the one my grandmother wore every day over the bun of hair she gathered on the back of her head. All the Brethren women of her generation wore their hair so, and all wore prayer coverings the year round. Mother, who had bobbed her hair in college, wore hers only for Love Feast and Communion, when I was expected to do the same. The assembled women and girls busied themselves removing their shoes and hiking up their dresses and slips to release nylon stockings held up by garter belts. There were several rows of gray metal folding chairs, with a basin of water and towels at one end. Whoever sat at the end of the row was the first to wash her neighbor's feet, who then did the same for her neighbor, and so on down the line until the last woman came up the line carrying the basin and towel, to wash the feet of the first. It's really hard to roll nylons over damp feet and even harder to pull the delicate fabric far enough up your thigh to hook it into garter belt tabs. You hardly need reminding that I hated nylons and garter belts. I have a jumbled memory of dark dresses, sensible shoes, and varicose veins blooming purple. The whole event of the Love Feast, and especially the foot washing, felt coercive to me. I was obligated to go, no matter what I wished, and I resented it even as I could barely formulate what I was feeling. I knew we were to think of our Savior's humility and service to others and feel inspired to humble ourselves in imitation of Him. I rebelled in my heart against any affective imperative, especially as it was reinforced by my mother. I think I was just sullen.

The Love Feast afterward was less harrowing. Mostly it was boring. The ham salad sandwiches of my childhood were no longer served, replaced by food undistinguished enough that I have no memory of what we ate. I just know that there was none of the glorious abundance of a different sort of church event, a covered-dish dinner where you could eat all the chicken *and* meatloaf, creamed corn *and* mashed potatoes, Jell-O *and* chocolate cake that you wanted. No such luck with the Love Feast. A Sunday school class served the food, and there was neither Jell-O nor cake. So the food was boring, and the service was boring, and I was fast becoming a bored and alienated teenager.

* * *

Decades later, I can nonetheless appreciate the foot washing in Kirsten and Matt's wedding, because it dramatizes values I still honor. The rituals of Love Feast and Communion help to create a community of faith, set apart from the thoughtless materialism of "getting and spending [that] lay waste our powers" and in opposition to the militarized state.[1] One time when I was in college, I returned home and came downstairs to find Mother at the kitchen table with tears in her eyes, reading the magazine *Sojourners*. It's published by a group of believers who go by that name, an intentional, evangelical community in Washington, D.C., that lives simply and communally, works on behalf of the weak and the poor in the District of Columbia, and lobbies for the least of these on Capitol Hill. "I sometimes wish," she said to me, "that I had dedicated my life to Christ as the Sojourners have. I sometimes think I have too much and have done too little." Not until Mother died did I read an inscription in her Bible that she had written when eighteen years old:

My Covenant
Lord, I give up all my own plans and purposes, all my own desires and hopes and accept Thy will for my life. I give myself, my life, my all utterly to Thee to be Thine forever. Fill me and seal me with Thy Holy Spirit. Use me as Thou wilt, send me where Thou wilt, work out Thy whole will in my life at any cost, now and forever.

Jane Miller
June 29, 1935

Lest this suggest to you a woman who thought more of the next world than this one, I hasten to add that Jane delighted in sensual pleasures—the taste of food, the beauty of fabrics, the joy of music, and was frank about the fact that she and Ken enjoyed sex—though, thankfully, she shared no details with me. Yet she did all her life seek to serve others and serve the Lord.

Seeking to witness for peace in a violent world, in her early sixties Mother founded with two others a Huntingdon chapter of the Pennsylvania Prison Society, an organization begun in Philadelphia by Quaker activists in the eighteenth century. The state prison in Huntingdon is one of the oldest, with high brick walls, round watchtowers, and fencing topped with multiple rolls of razor wire. In my Huntingdon life, I had driven by it thousands of times without considering what it was, and now it became one of the most significant institutions in Mother's life. She began to work on behalf of prisoners while Dad was still alive, and continued to for many years after his death. I think the relations she formed with imprisoned men and their loved ones were among the most important of her active older age. For fifteen years she visited prisoners, helped them communicate with the outer world, and sheltered in her home women who came out from the city with no money to pay for a motel room when visiting their imprisoned lovers, brothers, sons, and husbands. Together with her guest, she would put sheets and blankets on the foldout loveseat in Dad's study, and show them the downstairs powder room. She developed a special relationship with men sentenced to life imprisonment without parole, and met frequently with their support group. She truly believed in penitence, believed that we all need forgiveness and that we are all God's children. When asked by a journalist from the Huntingdon *Daily News* what motivated and sustained her years of activism, she said simply, "God's love."

My father's commitments were more unabashedly partisan. He characterized himself as an "unreconstructed New Dealer," ran for and was elected to the city council, wrote fully elaborated, multisyllabic letters to the editor of the newspaper, and talked with great animation about the issues of the day. Mother's contribution was less explicitly political. She was the chairman (*sic*) of the Huntingdon League of Women Voters for years, attended their national conventions, advocated for equality for women, and encouraged open exchange of political points of view. They supported the civil rights movement, and opposed the war in Vietnam. On this evidence, some people in town said they were Communists. They were in fact registered Democrats—which was practically the same thing.

* * *

How could I not be proud of my family and their values? My college friends said they wished their parents were like mine, and I could understand why. My Swarthmore lover's family is Southern Baptist, and when she came out her mother cried to her, "Oh, I wish you had just told me you were a prostitute. That would be so much better." My parents were by contrast practically saints. They suffered my rebellious teenage years, and embraced me when I came home from college a radical lesbian. In fact, they told me that they were pretty sure of my homosexuality before I made my formal announcement to them in my sophomore year, and in retrospect I can see that I declared myself evidently if not overtly when I tumbled into lustful love at age seventeen, while still living at home.

I told my parents everything, almost. I reserved my conviction that patriarchy could be undone only by radical feminists, who were, in my experience, mostly white lesbians. I didn't mention that I thought of myself as a radical scornful of bourgeois commitments and comforts. At Swarthmore, I helped to create a politicized community drenched in sexual desire and radical aspiration, talking the language of revolution. Swarthmore Women's Liberation and Swarthmore Gay Liberation were committed to fighting a patriarchy that seemed so universally pervasive that it permeated the very air we breathed, and a normatively heterosexual world that was boring, oppressive, unimaginative, and unattractive. I've long since learned the hard lessons that my lesbian feminist politics were racist and blind to the structural divisions of class. But in that moment I was caught up in working toward an unknown future that was tremendously exciting to me and my white friends. My schoolwork was truly challenging and I thrived in Swarthmore's college culture, which valued intellectual work above all else. What a relief! I was finally being rewarded for doing what came naturally, reading and writing about books, and kissing and caressing girls.

None of this seemed to faze my parents. They embraced me and they embraced my friends and lovers. At the remove of many decades, I've realized that I'd probably have been better off had my parents' response to my younger radicalism separated me from them a bit. A close friend at Wesleyan, who has two grown children, once told me that when her son was in college and studying abroad, he called home with news intended to shock. He reported that he'd just shaved his head (at a time when punk rock was ascendant). Both Ann-Lou and Michael let the remark pass unnoticed. Shortly after he got off the phone, Ann-Lou suddenly burst out, "We've got to call him back! You've got to yell at him for that—that's what he expected you to do and he's right." So Michael called him back, and told him he'd just done something stupid, immature, and disrespectful. Then all was well.

In my case, Huntingdon remained the referent for "home" until long, long after I graduated from college, and I made my own life while being pliant to parental expectations when I visited, faithfully attending church every Sunday and singing a grace before meals. I believed then and believe now that I could have caused them no more exquisite pain than by declaring my lack of faith and unwillingness to practice a religion I no longer believed. Whether in the end it would have been better if I had spoken out, I truly don't know. But I do fear I was not true to myself for much of my adult life as I became (for all intents and purposes) "Brethren" only in the company of my family. The fact remains that I kept my counsel, and found myself mentally assuming the posture of the Heisman Trophy when I was in Huntingdon or Lititz, doing an emotional stiff-arm to ward off family life, though I loved them all.

I was in graduate school, mid-twenties, when Mother called. "Tina, there's going to be a convening of Brethren women down at Bridgewater College—you know, the Brethren college in Virginia. It's going to happen this summer, in July, and we want to have a discussion of homosexuality. I thought you'd be the perfect person to lead the conversation. Could you come?" While the Church of the Brethren is a dissenter from the militaristic state and discounts the blandishments of the world, it is by no means radical when it comes to gender and sexuality. The importance of family life is assumed, as is the quietly patriarchal structure of that social unit, as David Watt demonstrates in his luminous, understated book *Bible-Carrying Christians*.[2] One of the congregations he studies is an Anabaptist church. The Mennonites who worship there are drawn to witnessing against war and living very simply, in the spirit of the witnessing that Mother found so attractive in the Sojourners. No member of that church, however, thought unremarkable, unexamined father-headed family life could be anything but good. There is no Brethren publication similar to the book published in 1963 by British Quakers, *Towards a Quaker View of Sex*, which argues that neither gender nor sexual orientation matters when considering loving relationships, but rather tenderness, responsibility, and commitment. Not all Quakers affirm that view even now, I'm sure, but there it was, a slim book among others on homosexuality that Swarthmore Gay Liberation demanded the college library buy, and one of the only ones—other than publications hot off the presses of Firebrand or just released by Shameless Hussy press—to represent homosexuality positively. In the last fifty years, much has been said about sexuality at the annual meetings of the Church of the Brethren, but the church has not been able to declare that *sexual orientation doesn't matter to God*—or to the Brethren, for that matter—let alone to welcome homosexuality as part of God's plan. In fact, the issue has repeatedly roiled Annual Conferences, and bitter words have been exchanged amid pleas for more temperate language.

I knew that the convening of Brethren women was of real importance to Mother—I even appreciated that she wanted that discussion of homosexuality. She believed with all her heart in tenderness, responsibility, and commitment, and loved her lesbian daughter without reserve. "Yes," I said, bowing before filial piety, even as I thought oh no, no, no. When the time came, I drove from Rhode Island as far as Washington, D.C., where I stayed with my lover from Swarthmore days and got really drunk girding my loins for the morrow. The next morning was blazing hot. I stopped for coffee at a neighborhood McDonald's, and drove down to southern Virginia, in July, in my car with no air conditioning, with a breakfast sandwich and an aching hangover. When I reached Bridgewater College, the air was oppressive with heat and humidity. Conference participants were housed in a college dorm, also with no air conditioning—and no fans. We ate dinner in the stifling college cafeteria, and later I lay awake for a long, long time in my narrow bed. The next day the hangover was gone and I led the workshop, and the day after that a final prayer ended the proceedings. Mother embraced me with tears in her eyes, saying, "Oh, I so wish Ken were here! I'm so proud of you." She thought he would be proud, too. I was happy in the moment— It's Over!—and pleased that people I cared about had witnessed my skills as a teacher, but mostly I wanted out. Out and away. It seemed absurd—me, a *Brethren lesbian*! But of course, I am.

* * *

Wesleyan's affiliation with Methodists seems to have left only an architectural trace, a lovely brownstone chapel, and I've never set foot there or anywhere else to attend a worship service. I don't go around calling myself Brethren, because I'm not. Yet as is patently obvious, we can't choose our families of origin, and we can't choose our childhoods, so I have no choice but to "be" Brethren. I am a professor, as my parents both were before me, and I've lived close to the campus, as my parents chose to do. I thought that the familial Anabaptism of my childhood had inclined me toward the professoriate, but no further. I now know otherwise. For better and for worse, I am my parents' daughter.

I may have held myself aloof from the Anabaptists, but the Anabaptists are nevertheless a part of me, and my desires are, in some queerly feminist way, Anabaptist desires. I want a complexly relational life and wish to help others, and over the years I created a far-flung network of elective affinities. This network distributed the overwhelming weight of caring for me, and made it possible for me to return home rather than go to a nursing home when discharged from rehab. Close friends helped with the overwhelming needs of my utter dependency, yet the filaments of the network also reached deep into Wesleyan as an institution. I had the accident the day before trustees were coming to Wesleyan, so they arrived twenty-four hours into the crisis. Three months later, they donated $8,000 toward the wheelchair that I still use—it's the right model for me, but wasn't covered by insurance. A vice president met Janet at the hospital very early the second day after the accident, to learn what information about my condition he could release in an e-mail message to all faculty and administrators. Only a few weeks earlier I had presided over the first faculty meeting of the year, where newly hired members of the faculty are introduced, so practically everybody knew who I was. The publicity of the accident—amplified by its timing—mattered, I'm sure, especially in the first days and weeks, but the sustained attention and care given to me over months and years responded to my own deep conscious and unconscious desires for connection to others.

In the horrific ordeal that followed my accident, Janet and I were saved first by the active love and generosity of our closest friends, but we needed more, and more was forthcoming. I was still quite ill from the shock of the damage to my central nervous system when I was discharged. I couldn't shift my weight at all when I was sitting in my wheelchair, which I did from noon to around 8:00 in the evening. So friends came over to cover the time when Janet was out of the house and tipped me from side to side every half hour to change the pressure points on my sit bones. I joked with Lori, who helped me generously hour after hour, saying I had become "a clown with sand in my head," the opposite of those inflatable punching clowns weighted at the bottom so that they pop right back up after being hit—because I found it difficult to stay upright at all. Yet, owing to her loving friendship and the help of so many others, I never had a pressure sore. Janet and I were fed for a full two years with lasagnas, quiches, curries, beans and rice, soups, brownies, and more lasagnas, all dropped off on the back porch, where half of the table was given over to washed casserole dishes, pie plates, and Tupperware we were returning. Janet would have wasted away without that food when I was in the hospital, I think, because she truly was then at a loss in the kitchen, and when I came home we were both overwhelmed. I did outpatient physical therapy at the Hospital for Special Care for a year and a half, five days a week, driven there and back by friends, an hour and a half commitment. I never missed a single therapy session. My friends were driving a second-hand van with a ramp and wheelchair tie-downs, which we paid for by drawing on the Christina Crosby

Fund that friends had set up at a local bank. Our household has stabilized, and our finances are no longer in the red every month, so we are no longer living on charity, but I'm honored that my friends gave freely to me in my time of great need. *Caritas* is, after all, "the highest love or fellowship," according to George Eliot.[3]

The Wesleyan community that supported me was heterogeneous and by no means of one mind on institutional questions. In the years before I got hurt, queer students would spend the night before National Coming Out Day "chalking," which entailed writing ribald messages in colored chalk on sidewalks all over the campus. One year a friend gleefully reported to me that someone had written "Christina Crosby's leather pants make me wet" on the sidewalk in front of the English Department, a message he saw when he came to his office early in the morning. Building and grounds workers soon scrubbed away that message and others less pointedly directed but no less enthusiastically expressed on the sidewalks all over campus. The students who covered the sidewalks with sexual vulgarities had high hopes their messages would *épater la bourgeoisie*, and they did. Many professors and members of the staff disliked the overnight flowering of unabashed, hyperbolically sex-positive assertions, but I was flattered by being so singled out. I knew that these sexually explicit messages were a way for the queer and "questioning" students to come together and act out, act up, and make Wesleyan theirs for a moment. I was all for it, and enjoyed the chalked-up, sexed-up Wesleyan they modified with their youthful, dissonant dissent, and the hopefulness of queer possibility. President Bennet was not of my opinion. He was offended by the annual ritual, and made an executive decision to ban the practice, asserting that the messages were offensive and explicit violations of community norms governing public discourse. I miss the chalking. It was ludic and unsubtle, unsuitable and excessive, and meant to be so. It let in air and light.

At the huge party we finally threw to thank all who helped us, after Janet's words of gratitude, Doug spoke up to testify that when any of the more conservative trustees would in conversation raise the topic of gay marriage, he was quick to say that he'd never seen a married couple more devoted to each other than Janet and I, proving that gay people could enter into matrimony as seriously as anyone else. Janet did not jump up to refute him, nor did I, because we were each deeply grateful for all that he and Midge had done for us, and recognize that it's impossible to square the circle of queer desire and sexually normative, corporate life. The community that kept us going was heterogeneous, created in response to my desire for connection with others, and included some who explicitly disagreed with each other, as Janet and I disagreed with Doug. It was a network connected to University life but distinct from Wesleyan as an institution. I felt no need to respond with thanks to God when I learned that the minister of the Congregational church and his parishioners prayed for me, but I felt sustained by their attention, nonetheless. When Dick asked whether Marxist prayers would help or hinder recovery, I said they'd help.

Lines of affiliation linked us to lesbians, gay men, and others thoroughly gender queer, and spun out to some who are married and apparently quite normal. The network included big city New Yorkers and small-town Pennsylvanians, multiple racial and national identifications, dear friends and people I didn't know face to face. All buoyed me up when "the waters came into my soul; I sank in deep mire: I felt no standing: I came into deep waters; the floods overflowed me."[4]

16

✳

Pretty, Witty,
and Gay

When Janet got to the hospital, she was asked several times whether I had been drinking before the accident. No, she said, I had not. She was asked again. "No, I already told you—she was riding her bicycle!" Then she was told that the question of alcohol had to be seriously addressed because of how it interacts with other drugs. A patient coming into the emergency room can be dangerously over-dosed on anesthesia and heavy-duty painkillers if she arrives with a lot of alcohol in her bloodstream. They also wanted to know if I was a heavy drinker addicted to alcohol, because, if so, they would keep the alcohol level in my blood high, so that I wouldn't experience withdrawal on top of the trauma of the accident. Janet assured them that this was not necessary, and after my first round of surgical anes-thesia, they reported to her that I must not do any drugs, because it didn't take much to keep me under.

A couple months before, coming up on my fiftieth birthday, I had gone to my general practitioner for a physical. Handed a ques-tionnaire about my alcohol consumption, I indicated that I drank one or two drinks every day, as I had done for decades, beginning in graduate school, and usually consumed more during the week-end. After my physician had completed the physical exam, she left me to get dressed and then returned with a sheaf of papers in her hand, including the questionnaire. That's when I learned that I was a "problem drinker." So I told Janet when I got home, "Guess what? I'm a problem drinker," and we puzzled over the apparent irrationality of rationalized medicine. The appellation seemed to both of us oddly misplaced. I hadn't experienced the sorts of problems either of us associated with "problem drinking"—missed work, car accidents, embarrassing outbursts. Still, the conversation with my doctor also made me wonder whether alcohol was in fact a problem in a way that I didn't clearly see. And if there was a problem, what was it?

Janet did not object to my drinking. In fact, even though she herself was an exceedingly moderate drinker—one glass of wine often lasted her the evening and she did not drink every night—she liked alcohol. Janet thinks that drinking helped to save her life when she was an adolescent and young adult. She started drinking in ninth grade, and discovered early on that she felt better—a lot better—when under the influence. She drank hard and pretty recklessly, and kept it up her four years at Dartmouth, where college traditions support heavy drinking, especially in the fraternities that continue to dominate student social life at the college. Then she graduated, and moved to Washington, D.C., to work in a consulting firm where about a third of the partners were Dartmouth alums—the other two thirds had graduated from Wesleyan or Duke. Both Dartmouth and Wesleyan had been coed for less than a decade, so most of the men who were partners of the firm had attended exclusively male institutions, with male bonding rituals. They did plenty of drinking, which set the tone for everybody else—work really hard, and then drink to relax and have fun. Yet in a life-affirming perversity, when Janet turned twenty-one and could drink legally anywhere, she stopped drinking altogether. Alcohol was no longer making her feel good, especially in the mornings after she'd been at the bar the night before. So she stopped. Without the alcohol, she felt bad enough to seek out a therapist with whom to talk. Missing the lift that alcohol had provided, she was struggling. "Stop drinking," the therapist said, "you really need to stop drinking, it's a depressant." "I don't drink anymore." No, you really have to give it up, the therapist kept repeating—she seemed incapable of understanding that after years of steady, serious drinking, Janet had stopped because *alcohol no longer made her feel good*. She didn't quit going to bars with her friends, she just drank club soda when she got there. Alcohol wasn't the problem for her. The problem was feeling flat and increasingly disconnected from life.

I find Janet deeply attractive because she attends to the truth of emotions, and is clear about her commitment to feeling good. She also has the will to do the hard work of changing her life, if that's what's necessary. For many complex reasons, she's given a lot of years to talk therapy and "bodywork"—massage, craniosacral therapy, yoga, swimming, and now Pilates. We have a running joke about her commitment to "process," the direct discussion of affective truths. Working out, and working through relational life. We call this talking "making sausage," because all kinds of stuff goes into it. Process is also stereotypically a lesbian way of life. When someone is making a mess of his life, as happens all too often in this screwed-up world of ours, we observe that he's got to get more lesbian—he's not made enough sausage. We are both pretty thoroughly processed, and quite committedly lesbian.

Over time, Janet has helped me understand how people use alcohol to manage their emotions—that means me, too. I already knew that alcohol was an immediate and welcome relief from the anxiety of figuring out social interactions, and a way to stop working and start having fun. That's what I learned drinking with my new friends from Juniata who had jobs in Huntingdon for the summer of 1970. Kathy was old enough to legally buy the Southern Comfort we poured into 7 Up and ice and drank sitting out on the fire escape. When I went to Swarthmore, I happily got drunk at the Gay Liberation parties we held. There was a lot of marijuana around the dorms, and some psychedelic drugs, which I enjoyed, but of all the drugs, alcohol became my favorite. Turning the sky purple, as I did when tripping on LSD, was fun, but abating my anxiety and lubricating my social relations were a lot better, taken all in all. In graduate school, I learned that having a drink at the end of the day, while preparing and eating dinner, drained away worries about work and offered an unfocused and immediate release. So I started drinking every day, and didn't stop until I broke my neck. I really, really miss it. I found that drinking alcohol afforded opportunities to talk with people—at receptions, cocktail parties, and dinners—and relaxed me enough that I felt comfortable conversing with just about anybody. Janet is the one who told me that "connection" is the keyword of Crosby conversation. Alcohol helped me connect.

* * *

I discovered when I was sixteen that drinking helped me in my social and emotional uncertainties. By the time I was fifty, I felt something was missing on the days when I couldn't have something to drink, and I would always think ahead to pick up beer or wine so it would be in the house. I enjoyed drinking, except for the periodic problem of hangovers, which I was finding increasingly unpleasant. Even so, I would sometimes quite consciously choose at a party to suffer in the morning for the pleasures of intoxication at night. That word—intoxication—points to the problem. You've put *in*to your body a toxin, which is to say a poison. When at a party, I would often choose bourbon or scotch, because I liked the taste and liked how distilled liquor worked, quickly spreading warmth and well-being.

So was I or was I not a problem drinker? Janet and I found the phrase curious, and in one way the anesthesiologist's report confirmed that opinion—I had no alcohol in my bloodstream when my broken body was delivered to the emergency room. But even though this quantitative measure showed that I was drinking moderately enough to pass the alcohol out of my system, it's no answer to the qualitative question about my psychic relation to drink. I find that the word, "addicted," does, in fact, speak to me—it names precisely how alcohol works. "Latin *addictus*, 'given over,' . . . *ad-*, to + *dicere*, to say, pronounce, adjudge."[1] "Given over"—you are dictated to. Alcohol told me that I was pretty, witty, and gay. So instructed, I could put aside whatever was troubling me and relax, and its dictates were compelling.

When I was drinking, I happily anticipated cocktail parties and receptions at Wesleyan. Janet reports that she noticed me at the women's studies beginning-of-the-year reception that I hosted at the little house I rented from the university, on a leafy cul-de-sac behind a dorm. She was at the Center for the Humanities for the year and completely new to Middletown. When I saw her come in, I went over to welcome her, glass of wine in hand. I recalled that the former director of the Center for the Humanities had mentioned that he had enjoyed a conversation with her about Methodists. He was by the fireplace talking to another of my friends, so I brought Janet over to include her in the conversation. Suddenly Natasha lurched to one side, grabbing at the mantle—the heel on one of her 1950s-era Dalmatian-patterned pumps had suddenly bent. "Wait a minute," I said with decisiveness, "I've got a vise grip in the basement. Let me see if I can fix it." Even though my dashing effort entirely failed to mend the shoe, Janet closely observed the whole scene and correctly deduced that I liked tools and liked to charm girls in high heels.

She also decided that I was flirtatious, and she was right. Most of the time, flirting was a kind of leavening agent that encouraged conversation to expand. It's light, bright, inconsequential, insignificant. Girls just want to have fun, oh, oh, oh, girls just want to have fun. Yet if alcohol dictates a desire for pleasure, I discovered when I first began drinking at Juniata that for me it was often the pleasure of sexual desire, and desire mixed with alcohol is seemingly irresistible and imperative. Time slows down to the present moment, and the expansive, consequential world of the sober and responsible is lost to view. It just doesn't matter—then. Alcohol alone cannot effect this eclipse, but alcohol urges concentration on now and foreshortens perspective. My college years ran alcohol and sex together in unsurprising ways. The stakes were considerably higher in my fully adult life, when I used drinking to help me flirt seriously—not an oxymoron—because I was stoking and yielding to desires I knew would make real trouble, and not only for me. I pursued such flirtations despite the fact that I was in a presumptively monogamous, long-term relationship. Now *that's* a problem. I wanted the settled, home-sharing, loving, long-term relationship that I had, yet I also wanted to take my distance and live drenched in exciting newness and urgent desire. My adventures were now and again by no means innocent, and I regret the pain so liberally spread about when I played out my deep ambivalence about domesticity and desire. I was, in fact, a problem drinker insofar as alcohol allowed me to sustain this emotional contradiction for years—I couldn't have done it without the way alcohol grays out the deliberations of conscience.

At Wesleyan, the drinking that was part of the culture at the Center for the Humanities suited me just fine. The Monday night lectures at the Center for the Humanities were often preceded by drinks and dinner, and followed by a coffee-and-cookies reception. Then the fellows and the fellow travelers would gather at someone's home for an after-party, where there was always plenty to drink. Janet observed that all of the social events of the Center, where we both held fellowships in 1996–1997, were geared to seeing how well you held your alcohol, which makes sense, given that the Center had been at the height of its fortunes and flush with money in the 1950s, when white men (and Hannah Arendt) sat around writing papers, talking among themselves, and drinking and smoking as a matter of course. Smoking has largely disappeared from my world. I have in my office a glass ashtray with a profile view of John Wesley in the center, a relic of bygone days, now a convenient place to toss my keys. The Center, on the other hand, is still fully stocked with liquor, ranged on shelves in a large closet. Thinking and talking about ideas excited me, and alcohol encouraged my conversation and burnished my thoughts. That culture of socializing through drinking held firm for decades, and I found it a lovely, even delicious social medium. Janet and I pitched headfirst into love at the Center for the Humanities, which had also been the scene of other erotic adventures of mine, affairs that ended badly, hurt others, and left me guilty, heartsick, and bereft. Yet they had begun readily enough in the alcohol-enriched atmosphere and intellectual exchanges of the Center.

My problem drinking stopped when Janet and I got together. Actually, that's not quite true, I realize, because the worst fight she and I ever had was fueled by alcohol, and is the only time in my drinking life that I ever blacked out and couldn't recall what had happened when I woke up the next morning. I felt physically wretched and emotionally sick—what the hell had I done? To make what could be a long story short, Janet and I had gone to Huntingdon to visit Mother. With Janet's help, I had gathered myself to tell Mother that we were not going to sleep over in her one-bedroom apartment, but had a motel room across town on Route 22—a reasonable position, since I knew that we otherwise would be sleeping in her double bed and she would be out in the living room on a small sofa. In order to nerve myself for that moment of saying "no" to my mother and making room, quite literally, for myself with Janet, I drank as I cooked and continued drinking as we ate. When that moment came, Mother was confused and distressed, as I feared she would be. My family valued togetherness above all else, so the idea that I might value time alone with Janet in the midst of a family visit did not, could not, make sense to my mother. "We'll be more comfortable in our own room, especially since Jake takes a long time to wake up in the morning," I tried to explain. "I'll come here to have breakfast with you, and Janet'll join us at lunch." Then we left. In the morning, I vaguely remembered that leave-taking, but had no memory of what followed. "You started fighting as soon as we got in the car," Janet informed me. "You were drunk and belligerent, downright hostile, and I told you so. You kept it up when we got to the motel. I said I was done talking to you and went to bed. So did you, and you were out like a light."

Now *that's* problem drinking. When I woke up, though I couldn't recollect any of the details, I knew I had acted very badly. The disinhibiting effects of alcohol clearly had allowed me to both feel and express my anger at needing to leave my mother, which I also desperately wanted to do. A far cry from pretty, witty, and gay.

Fighting scares me, so my apologies were pretty abject. Janet is not one to stick around for abuse, so I consider myself fortunate that she didn't pack it in then and there, but she reasoned that she had never before seen me act badly when drunk. We nonetheless had to work through what had happened that night, which took considerably longer than a day or two. That long, recursive conversation was focused largely on my relation to my family, and especially to Mother, a long reckoning spelled out in this account of myself. About drinking, we agreed that for the most part it helped me to be relaxed, talkative, flirtatious, and fun loving, and wasn't itself a point of conflict. Over time, we figured out how to fight productively, and I didn't again use drink to steel myself as I had done to leave my mother, though the big question of how I continued to depend on alcohol remained open.

So the misery of that night passed away. We're now able to joke about the Huntingdon Motor Inn, where every room was furnished with a flyswatter, and outside the office two vending machines sat side by side, one selling Coca-Cola and the other live bait.

* * *

When Janet got her job in New York City, and we were in Middletown for the summer, we decided to have a party, and determined it should feature a cocktail paired with a lawn game, the more incongruous the better—martinis and horseshoes, for instance. We told our guests to "dress appropriately," leaving it to them to decide on the leading event. Some came in their slinky silk sophisticated best, while others wore old blue jeans and sneakers, prepared for the horseshoe pit. The horseshoe pitching picked up as afternoon turned into evening. Dick offered play-by-play coverage of the action, bringing to horseshoes the exacting detail of baseball announcing. In the end, when it had grown so late that a tipsy partygoer could easily throw a wild pitch, he declared a final victor, and awarded the garishly golden, plastic martini-glass trophy in a brief but moving ceremony. The winner? An eminence in the field of queer studies, who could not remember a single sporting contest he'd won before.

In Henry's victory remarks to the crowd, he noted that the competition had been fierce—his defeated rival was a visibly pregnant woman in a short black dress, wearing high heels. I had a blast, and then a parched hangover when I woke up the next morning. No matter. What I remember is the summer sun filtered through the canopy of trees, the taste of the cocktails, the comedy of the games, and the pure joyful fun of it all.

In my two decades at Wesleyan before I broke my neck, I had worked with colleagues I both liked and respected, and with whom I elaborated a social life of drinking, dinners, and parties. That was the happy part of my drinking, which most of the time felt not like a problem but a pleasure. Betsy, who lived one street over, is a very accomplished cook and hosted some of the most memorable events. To get to her parties after evening lectures, I cut through a neighbor's back yard, and there I was. I ate and drank and talked so many times in her house that I can see vividly before me the scene in her dining room—a big oval table laden with her gorgeously prepared and savory ham, surrounded by patés, bowls of jerkins and olives, fragrant cheeses, and sliced baguette. Bottles of liquor and various wines were set out just beyond in the kitchen, the refrigerator was full of Anchor Steam beer, and the counters littered with the half-empty glasses of a party in full swing. The rooms were crowded with partygoers and loud with conversation. I had such fun.

A few years ago, Betsy invited me to a party she was hosting to celebrate the promotion of one of her colleagues. I hadn't been in her house since I broke my neck. I remembered a concrete stoop with steps, so I arranged for my friend MJ to help me get in. When I was outside, I called her on my cell phone. She came out and got from the back of the van the extendable ramps that I carry around, and set them up at the right width for my wheels. We got the wheelchair up the steps and bumped me over the threshold, into the vestibule—

just barely, because the room was packed. There I stayed. The living room was loud and crowded with people. The rooms beyond—and the food and drink—were utterly inaccessible to me. Right away, Betsy came over to welcome me, and quickly returned with a glass of wine. So, too, some friends made their way through the crowd to say hello, including my newly tenured friend. I was so happy for her! Someone retrieved for me a little plate of food, as delicious as ever. Increasingly free laughter and talk came from the crowded rooms, and, sitting there, stuck just inside the front door, the *party* felt largely inaccessible to me, despite my ramps. I left after about an hour and went home sober and sad.

*　*　*

Soon after I returned to work half-time, teaching one course a semester and slowly picking up my research and writing, I read a smashingly intelligent book, *The Ideas in Things*, by Elaine Freedgood. She details how the material things that proliferate in nineteenth-century British novels speak to us of imperial power and the furnished interiors of Victorian psychic life. The darkly polished old mahogany furniture of the red room where Jane Eyre is imprisoned by the vindictive Mrs. Reed, for example, reappears when Jane redecorates rooms in St. John's Moor House. This latter furniture Freedgood calls "a souvenir of sadism," recollecting *both* the destruction of the forests and implementation of plantation slavery in Madeira and the Caribbean *and* the sadistic torments Jane endured at Gateshead.[2] I wrote a review of the book, my first post-accident publication. I also recommended to my colleagues in the English Department that we bring the author for a colloquium. Elaine and I spoke together briefly in my office before the event, and then, as I sat directly facing her at the end of the seminar table, I struggled against sleep—and lost. Again and again my eyes closed, and again and again I jerked awake. As you know, I take OxyContin against pain, and I will continue to take it despite the fact that it slows down my whole system. I was nodding off, to use the phrase we associate with heroin, which is what the opiate addicts turn to when the pharmaceutical stuff is out of reach. When the seminar was over, I got in my van to go downtown to the restaurant where I had reserved seats for the speaker, several of my colleagues, and myself. The key simply clicked. Nothing. The battery to the van was dead, which happens all too often because the adaptive technology continually draws down energy. The van had nodded off, too.

Instead of joining my colleagues for the colloquium dinner, where there'd be drinking, eating, and talking, the very sort of gathering that once gave me such pleasure, I called with my apologies. Thank God the battery was dead so that I had a truthful excuse, because I was simply mortified that I had fallen asleep in the face of the speaker. More than embarrassed, I suffered what felt like a kind of social death, as the word "mortification" suggests. I was miserable. I'm well aware that this event doubtless mattered very little to others. That did not then, nor does it now, assuage my bitter sense that a way of living I highly valued and actively enjoyed is no longer fully available to me. I've learned to take a thermos of coffee with me to lectures, and (impolitely) drink it during the talk to avoid the misery of heavy eyelids and a heavy head, and have managed to stay awake and even join the discussion.

That's a far cry, however, from the fun I used to have when warmed by alcohol and the excitement of ideas. I don't know whether I ever would have decided that responding to alcohol bound me to the drug so tightly as to distort my life. I never came to that reckoning. The world has also changed around me, and I don't know how I would have participated in the Wesleyan of the new millennium had I not broken my neck. I only know that as I drink wine oh-so-moderately, I miss martinis. I miss Manhattans. I miss our cocktail parties. I miss the ease that came when I drank, and the social connections and excitement that alcohol facilitated. Alcohol no longer dictates to me, and rather than the happy assurance that I'm pretty, witty, and gay, I hear nothing, or only the vaguest murmur.

17

✳

The Horror! The Horror!

Years before my accident, I was sitting in my study preparing to teach George Eliot's novel *The Mill on the Floss* to the thirty-two students in my course titled Reading the Victorians. Tears were running down my cheeks, and I knew that I wanted the students to understand how words on a page could elicit such strong emotion. So I worked that afternoon to teach the class how the conventions of realism project a space-time populated with "round" characters whose imagined lives we follow, often with real interest. We discussed how the happenings of this fictional world can move readers even when—or perhaps especially when—melodramatic conventions intrude. *The Mill on the Floss* is the second of Eliot's eight novels, written before she had fully mastered the genre, so the opening scenes prefigure somewhat too heavily the tragedy that will overtake the novel's passionate heroine, Maggie, who conforms only with difficulty and great inward effort to the narrow dictates that tell her how to be a good girl. The conclusion is flawed, too, veering close to melodrama as the heroine's virtues—manifestly evident to us throughout, but unrecognized by those she loves—are at last witnessed by her upright and judgmental brother, Tom, just moments before they are together overwhelmed by the waters of a great flood she has braved to rescue him. "In their death they were not divided." It's a story about a brother and sister, so of course I was moved. Melodramatic tactics work, and I was crying not only over the death of the heroine, but over missed chances to overcome the painful distance from her brother, the impossibility of turning back the flow of time so that Maggie's life could be different, the impossible regret of "if only" so central to melodrama.

What one scholar has called the "realist consensus" upholds the widely shared belief in the morally complex characters realist conventions create, characters whose depths are accommodated by the expansive, three-dimensional space in which they appear.[1] We take "depth of character" for granted, as characters repeatedly display the attributes that we recognize as belonging to them, seen first from this angle and then that, which is one of the reasons that Victorian novels are a pleasure to read. A masterful writer like Eliot can create and populate a whole town and its environs. Her narrators encourage readers to pass moral judgments, though with a writer as accomplished as Eliot, we're not readily tempted to become moralistic and imagine ourselves above it all. So even when a novel governed by the realist consensus takes a melodramatic turn and ends tragically, as happens in *The Mill on the Floss*, the narrative has created an ordered imaginative world where my mind can rest, and characters whose contradictions I can understand.

Realism progresses through chronologically sequential time toward a knowable future, and creates an imagined world you find continuous with your own. Most importantly, the realist consensus urges certain beliefs, perhaps most importantly the idea that "we" are all complexly motivated, but knowable human beings, fundamentally alike. I have grave reservations about such beliefs, which presuppose history as progressive and unified in space and time—imagined from a European point of view, of course, since Europe is clearly where humanity is furthest advanced. These premises are contradicted by the world we live in. I know that the "realist consensus" does not produce novels that "reflect real life." Rather, a comprehendible world is conjured by the imagination of an artist, illuminated by the austere, searching light of the Anglo-European Enlightenment, and laid out on the premises that history progresses organically and that we all belong to the family of man. Knowing how these books call upon readers to participate in the realist consensus and legitimate its claims does not, however, diminish my pleasure in entering into an imaginary world ordered according to its unspoken rules. To the contrary—it's a familiar and reassuring domain that offers the substantial comfort of knowing where I am, especially since I needn't believe what I read.

"Of course you have to begin with the preface!" I said decisively from the hospital bed where I was lying for a third day awash in the bright lights and encompassing whiteness of the intensive care unit. "You can't skip!" I was instructing Janet, who was sitting in a chair by my bedside, holding *Middlemarch* on her lap. Apparently I had asked for this book the previous day when I'd emerged from my induced unconsciousness, which suggests the hold that this novel has on my imagination. "You know it's a parable that situates the 'ardent' and 'theoretic' character of Dorothea—besides, there's the voice of that comprehensively instructive narrator!" (Several years before, Janet and I had gone to a conference on narrative form, where she met some of my Victorianist friends, and came away amused and impressed by my colleagues' belief that you must attend to every detail, down to the very syntax of Eliot's sentences.) So she began at the beginning. *Middlemarch* is Eliot's penultimate novel, and demonstrates her truly masterful control of realist conventions. No heavy-handed forecasting or "if only" regrets, just the slow accretion of detail that populates an imagined provincial manufacturing town and its surrounding countryside with a multitude of fully rounded characters and their intricate web of interactions over time.

I was so bewildered by my injuries and sedated by drugs that I have no memory of Janet reading aloud to me. I do know that when I got to the Hospital for Special Care, she borrowed from the public library in Middletown a twenty-three-cassette edition read by an accomplished speaker of British English. That way I could enter the imagined provincial world of Middlemarch when Janet was not there and I was not doing therapy, during the long, empty hours in the unimaginable world I had entered and the incomprehensible body I'd become. I was far better off in the Vincys' hospitable house, or the oppressively evangelical Mr. Bulstrode's office at the bank, or with young, vibrant Dorothea in the Lowick house of the Rev. Mr. Casaubon, where she is slowly coming to understand that her husband is far from the great divine she had imagined him to be. Day after day, I had only to patiently wait for the CNA to answer my call bell when I needed to have one cassette taken out and another put into the small boombox sitting on the table next to me.

* * *

The realist consensus is an achievement of Renaissance humanism and Anglo-European Enlightenment, and the world it represents is expansive, comprehensible, and rationally ordered. Not so the neurological storm of spinal cord injury. I was lost in its vastness and shades of unilluminated darkness, and in desperate need of familiar things. Of course I asked for *Middlemarch*! Given this fact, I can hardly fault memoirists who answer to the dictates of the realist consensus when writing about disability. Many accounts of living with a disabling incapacity begin at the beginning—the discovery at birth of a supposed "defect," the account of a genetic anomaly, diagnostic test, or catastrophic accident. The narrative develops chronologically after the advent of incapacity, all the while implicitly articulating events into a consequential order. Moving through time is simultaneously moving through space, of course, and that space is three-dimensional, oriented by a single vanishing point in the distance toward which the narrative moves as it develops. You conjure this space in your imagination as you read, and discover the common horizon that organizes the trajectories of all the characters, including yourself as you become absorbed in the story. You enter into the scenes and follow the incapacitated person as she seeks to regain lost abilities or discover new ones, and sympathize when she must persevere through setbacks and disappointments. Authors and audience alike rely on common sense, and the story moves sequentially from beginning to end.

From the very first pages, you are reading with the "anticipation of retrospection."[2] Readers attend to the details of the emerging narrative with the expectation that the author has organized his story to end with a satisfying sense of conclusion. Frank discussions of setbacks tend toward workable solutions and the discovery by the protagonist that he is, in fact, living his life—a difficult life, yes, and certainly different from what he had expected, but a life with its satisfactions and pleasures. The quadriplegic poet Paul Guest has written a memoir I admire, *One More Theory about Happiness*, in which he describes the blankness that followed from his terrible bicycle accident when he was thirteen, just on the verge of puberty. He does not shy from representing the dark moods and thwarted desires that inform his writing and shadow his growth into manhood and his development as a poet. The poem "My Index of Slightly Horrifying Knowledge" is a catalog of indignities large and small that I read with a wry, nearly bitter, laugh of recognition. Yet the narrative of his memoir, which begins in childhood and ends when he is engaged to be married, is motivated by his longing for a fully adult life, imagined as the familiar story of reciprocated heterosexual fulfillment. This happy narrative arc is at odds with the dark comedy of the horrifying knowledge he represents with an enviable poetic precision. A longing for heterosexual normalcy drives Guest's narrative, which in consequence I can't reckon as one *more* theory about happiness. Narratives of disability may be grim at some points, but they almost always move toward a satisfying conclusion of lessons learned and life recalibrated to accommodate, even celebrate, a new way of being in the world.

Nothing of the sort is happening here, because I can't resolve the intractable difficulties of disabling incapacity, any more than I can suggest that everything will be (more or less) okay. Even the most accomplished cripple you can imagine is undone, and living some part of her life in another dimension, under a different dispensation than that of realist representation. In my case, spinal cord injury casts a very long shadow, the penumbra of which will only grow darker as the years pass and the deficits of age begin to diminish me still further. I'm living a life beyond reason, even if I have invoked some of the stabilizing conventions of realism in this narrative. Those conventions are the ones I know best, but profound neurological damage actually feels to me more like a horror story, a literary genre governed not by rational exposition but rather by affective intensification and bewilderment.

*   *   *

In horror stories "the boundary between the real and the fictive, the interpretations of experience by the audience and the characters, is continually drawn and effaced," Susan Stewart writes in an essay on the epistemology of the genre. "Both the story and its context of telling dissolve into a uniformity of effect. Hence, the 'didn't really happen' of the fiction is transformed into a 'really happened,' a fear which is 'real,' yet which has no actual referent."[3] In other words, such a story depends on the feeling of fear that it evokes in its characters, and the simultaneous unease it engenders in you. Edgar Allan Poe's story "The Fall of the House of Usher" works this way. From the opening paragraph's "dull, dark, and soundless days of the year, when the clouds hung oppressively low in the heavens" to the "full, setting, and blood-red moon" of the end, Poe's first-person narrator inhabits a terrible world, and as you read, you discover that there's never a relief from the sense that something very bad is upon you.[4] Every element of the narrative is overcharged with significance, every detail mysteriously endowed with a blank surplus that oppresses rather than enlightens. Horror stories insist on this referential surplus to overwhelm our efforts to figure out what's going on. Such stories defy the cerebral undertaking they seem to encourage, because their meaning is affective, not referential. The fear they induce is the fear of fear itself.

In Poe's story, the unnamed narrator, who in his anonymity could be any one of us, begins the story as he is approaching the House of Usher, where he comes in response to the urgent call of an old friend who is terrified. Of what? He doesn't know, but the setting is desolately foreboding and the narrator increasingly uneasy. He attempts to soothe his friend, to no avail. His friend has a twin sister, but she is ill, and he glimpses her but once. "[T]he lady Madeline . . . passed slowly through a remote portion of the apartment and . . . disappeared. I regarded her with an utter astonishment not unmixed with dread—and yet I found it impossible to account for such feelings." After several gloomy days, her brother "informs him abruptly that the lady Madeline is no more." She has died—of what? We never know. His host fears her medical men, implying they would dig up the corpse for dissection, though the story affords meager evidence of this particular threat. It must be, he declares, interred in a crypt below the mansion. The men together do the work. The atmosphere of foreboding grows only stronger in the days following, and at last the narrator finds himself giving way to "unaccountable horror." As a wild storm whirls outside, he discovers his friend in a kind of trance, muttering that he's heard his sister alive in her coffin, when a great gust blows open the heavy door that communicates with the crypt. There she stands in her shroud with arms outstretched, his terrifying doppelgänger, only to pitch forward in her final agony into her brother's embrace. Her death calls for his, and both fall lifeless at the feet of the narrator. In great haste he leaves the mansion, and just in time, for as he looks back, a jagged fissure divides the House of Usher down the middle. "My brain reeled as I saw the mighty walls rushing asunder," he tells us, and "there was a long tumultuous shouting sound like the voice of a thousand waters—and the deep and dank tarn at my feet closed sullenly and silently over the fragments of the 'House of Usher.'" In this horror story, the brother and sister twins in their mimetic relationship terrify as René Girard says they must always do.

The tumultuous end leaves unanswered all causal questions, which actually never had purchase in the story, anyway. In a horror story, *how* the characters and events of the story are ordered and discussed collapses into the *what* of those events that gathers affective force. The result is generalized fear, a feeling that doesn't *refer* to anything real, but *is itself real*. From the title of "The Fall of the House of Usher" forward, we've been waiting for a collapse, an end that's reached as the narrator flees. The house first splits in two, a violent rending apart of what had been perversely conjoined, and is then entirely obliterated. Readers have been aligned throughout with the narrator by virtue of the first-person address to an implicit "you," and with him readers experience the fear of fear that amplifies into horror. This horror detaches the audience from the realm of the ordinary and precipitates us elsewhere.

* * *

I find myself repeatedly, daily, relentlessly, and wearyingly horrified by the elsewhere of spinal cord injury. All too often I feel as if I'm living in another world, a dark realm overshadowed by the life-threatening accident that didn't kill me, but obliterated the life I had been living and put me in a mimetic relationship to my brother. I'm advancing toward something that evokes horror in me, the referent of which is shrouded in a baleful mystery rendered more menacing as I proceed, my horror gathering as I realize that whatever "it" is, it has already happened, yet worse lies ahead. I'm not writing a horror story, I'm living one. In becoming Jeff's twin, my world was destroyed, and the terrifying aura of neurological destruction and paralytic incapacity encompassed me.

What is it I'm so afraid of? I've turned this over in my mind repeatedly, and think that I have some glimmer of what's at stake. I don't relive the day of the accident. The fact is, I don't remember anything about the accident itself. My memory stops about a half mile before the spot where the branch caught my spokes, pitching my bicycle sideways in an instant—in a nanosecond—so quickly that I arrived at the hospital with my chin obliterated, and not another scratch on me. My face was smashed and I broke my neck. Yet my fear is not retrospective, incessantly returning to the accident that so wrecked my life, but prospective. Something horrible awaits—the future. Life will go on, day after day, until I die. I fear getting older and bearing the trials of aging in my deeply compromised body. I fear living with interminable pain, both neuropathic and emotional, and I fear interminable grief. It colors the world and is just too hard sometimes to bear. I fear not death, but living.

Otto Kernberg, in a psychoanalytic account of the process of mourning, makes this observation:

> Daily reality militates against the full appreciation of a loving rela-
> tionship, and only retrospectively emerges the possibility of a perspec-
> tive that fully illuminates the potential implications of every moment
> lived together. The paradox of the capacity to only appreciate fully
> what one had after having lost it, a profoundly human paradox, can-
> not be resolved by communicating this experience to others. It is an
> internal learning process fostered by the painful, yet creative aspect
> of mourning.[5]

No. Damn it, no! I appreciated every moment of the life that Janet and I made together and I fully appreciated her. I knew what I had. I could not integrate my intellectual and sexual passions until I was forty-six, so all the more reason to be alert to the joys of daily life. Take the motorcycle, for example.

I had always wanted a bike, and bought a used Honda Nighthawk 750 in the first year of my life with Janet. It was a great bike. The world of motorcycles now breaks down into sport bikes with engines whining at really high RPMs and seats that pitch the rider aggressively forward into a racing position, versus low-slung cruisers with engines that rumble, the louder, the better. Cruisers put the rider in a cool laid-back position—think *Easy Rider*. The 1984 Nighthawk is what's called a hybrid, more of a sport bike, but with a bench seat that can accommodate a passenger. I happily rode it the fifty-mile round-trip to New Haven when I was in psychoanalysis—the only happy part of my analysis, I might add—but it wasn't really comfortable for Janet. To celebrate my fiftieth birthday, we decided to buy a bike that would be great for both rider and passenger. Looking around, I found a black Honda Shadow, a cruiser with great lines, the kind of bike I thought I wanted. But when I took it out for a ride, I didn't like how cumbersome it felt, with its wide handlebars and foot pegs set out in front. Leafing through the classifieds on a Sunday morning in spring 2003, we found the right bike—a black-and-silver Triumph with a lovely 900cc "speed triple" engine and the shorter turning radius and maneuverability of a sport bike, plus the lower carriage of a road bike. It had a seat contoured to carry a passenger, was highly polished, beautifully cared for, and looked brand-new. It even came with black leather saddle bags. When we went over to Poughkeepsie to get the motorcycle, I came back on Interstate 84 among the tractor-trailers, which reminded me of riding my bicycle in the scrum of taxis in New York City. I was proud of myself and loved the bike. I printed a photo from the Triumph website that showed it to perfection, and Janet had it hanging on the door to her office.

On September 2, my birthday, I had meetings in the morning, and went off to work carrying anxieties about my job that year as chair of the faculty, a highly visible position that burdened me with responsibility even as I was glad my colleagues thought well enough of me to vote me into it. When I returned home for lunch, my worries about work vanished. There was Janet, all proud and happy, dressed in a sexy, sleeveless black velvet top, a silver velvet skirt, and silver sandals. The garage door was open, showcasing the black-and-silver bike with black-and-silver wrapped gifts piled on it. A red ribbon accent picked up the thin red sporting stripe on the gas tank. The presents themselves were little things—on this occasion, the real gift was the presenter and presentation. I vividly remember how happy I was.

Photographs confirm that memory. We used to take pictures all the time, and recalled our pleasures as we put them into photo albums, where we have six years of happiness on page after page. One day a couple of years ago, wondering whether my memory had somehow burnished past happiness, I dared to search for the birthday photographs. Was I inflating in my memory the daily pleasures of my life with Janet and the moments of sheer joy that illuminated those days and years? I found the pictures seemingly untouched in their Mystic Photo Labs envelope. Flipping through them, I realized that I had not exaggerated my happiness, and that the photos fairly hum with merriment and desire.

I don't know if Janet's ever looked them over. I've never talked about it with her. We've certainly never gone through those photos together, as we used to do with each new envelope of negatives and prints, and I've looked at them only that once. They are still out in the living room. That envelope is somewhere. At this moment, eleven years after my accident, they still feel like green kryptonite to me. Dangerous, dangerous. Love, passion, giddiness, joy, pleasure, desire fairly burn through those photos and the ones arrayed in the albums that record six years of birthdays, holidays, and everyday adventures. There's no way to rewrite what happens, my lost body is forever lost, and I am forever reliving the events of the past that take on a dangerous golden glow. It's the glow of illuminated amber in which my remembered body is transfixed. Dr. Kernberg would have it that "the painful, yet creative act of mourning" will allow me to fully appreciate in retrospect what I've lost. This "internal learning process" is a concept so innocent of complexity that I really can't stand it. I knew what I had. I know what I've lost.

Besides, the analytic talk about grief is always focused on the relationship between the dead and the living. No one's dead in this case, although I often wished in the early months and years that the accident had killed me and sometimes still do. Janet got angry at me one evening after I'd been home a couple of months, as she was pushing the wheelchair toward the dining room that was serving as our bedroom. I had been worrying with my tongue what felt like a new tooth protruding from my gums just below my lower front teeth, and I wondered aloud what it could be. "It's probably a bone chip," Janet said, and I cried out, "I am so fucking fucked, I can't believe how fucked I am," thinking of my broken face pinned together by the surgeons and wondering what else would emerge. "What does that say about me?" Janet said, her voice rising, clearly pissed. "When you talk like that you're just erasing me and all the work I do, as if it were for nothing." Immediately scared, certainly because of my dependence on her, and perhaps contrite, I said I was sorry. But she went on, indignantly, "All my work, all my care . . . and me—it's as though I don't matter to you at all." I protested the contrary, and again apologized, saying that I'd think about her position. It's very true that I loved her dearly and was sorry to have hurt her.

"It's not just the labor—although that's part of it, for sure. There's something else, though, and it's this—You also overlooked—no, refused to see—negated—my love for you. You may not love your body, but I do—you should know by now that I want to be your physical lover. I'm working on understanding and accepting the fact that you do not love your body and, from the way you talk about it, it doesn't seem likely you ever will. But saying you're completely fucked is saying that my desire for you and my love is of no consequence." We were drinking our morning tea in bed, and Janet was describing how she'd felt the night before. As we talked, I came to understand the logic of her complaint, and from that moment forward I vowed not to break out in imprecations against my life, a life that is sustained by her considerable and absolutely necessary labor and even more by her loving regard. Yet on a bad day of pain and discomfort that abstracts and alienates me from my life, I feel my attachment to the world attenuate, and cannot contemplate aging, with its attendant physical and mental decline, with anything but horror. At such a moment, death turns a benignant aspect to me.

* * *

What is it about my injured life that militates against mourning and keeps grief fresh? What makes it feel like a horror story? In a horror story, you begin by being afraid, and all its devices are dedicated to stoking the fear of fear, making it clear that there's worse to come, that, if you're afraid now, you'll be terrified in a moment. When? Wait. Just you wait. You'll see. You'll see . . .

I'm afraid I'll stop grieving and equally afraid that I'll never stop grieving. If I *do* stop grieving, I will necessarily have come to terms with my profoundly changed body and my profoundly changed life, for I can leave off mourning only by no longer cherishing and burnishing my memories of the past.

I may be perverse, but I'm terrified of what I'll lose in making my peace with what I've lost. I fear I'm forgetting how it felt to be comfortable in my body as time does its wearing work. I fear I'm losing how my embodied passions felt through my whole body, and I'm afraid that I'll forget the feeling of joy.

If I *don't* stop grieving, and refuse to move on, I fear that I'll be always missing the body and the life I had at the moment I broke my neck. I'll be caught in the sticky resin of amber. New pleasures will be foreclosed. I fear being impossible to live with—and I fear not wanting to live.

18

✳

Living On

Yet here I am. I'm sitting at my desk, outlined by and suffused with neuropathic pain, that tingling, vibrating, burning sensation that I've been describing from the very beginning. The pain is uncomfortable—today, that's all. When I'm concentrating, my bodymind turns to the task at hand and this sensation becomes background, only to reassert itself as I lose focus and return, as it were, to my resting state. How am I to represent this complex embodied fugue? My skin is an organ of sense that runs imperceptibly from inside my body to the outside, or from outside to inside, which defeats the idea that I'm living *in* my body. There are 108 single-word prepositions in the English language, and none is adequate to representing the relation of mind to body. Body and mind are simultaneously one and the same and clearly distinct. Thinking my body, I am thinking in my body, as my body, through my body, of my body, about my body, and I'm oriented around my body. I'm beside myself. Perhaps the most powerful effect of the realist consensus is what Ermarth calls the "concordance of difference," the summing up at the end of a novel that's sometimes explicitly offered to the readers by an author, as Eliot apprises us of where and how her characters live on after the end of her story in *Middlemarch*. The more detail, the more exhilarating and exhaustive is the effort to orient it all toward a single vanishing point, and the more perspectives from which we see a character like Dorothea, the more she acts differently, but always like "herself." Differences multiply, but in the end they add up with no remainder. The account balances. My account doesn't. I can't make sense of this body, which continues to surprise and baffle me.

When I was first hurt, I began to feel a dense and obdurate need to put into words a body that seemed beyond the reach of language. I searched for words to describe to Doctor Seetherama phenomenological realities that made no sense to me, and tried to explain what I felt to the aides who were turning me in bed. I live on in a neurological storm—it's electric, even now sometimes violent enough to be overwhelming, and certainly endless enough to be horrifying. Yet my life is not in truth a horror story, and I have no wish to claim that it is, however powerfully that genre has helped me conceptualize my fear of the future.

I have lived on eleven years beyond the accident, through the suspension of life occasioned by terrible loss that Emily Dickinson represents with such fierce precision in her poem "After Great Pain." The experience may be so intense that it freezes rather than burns. Then death beckons.

> This is the Hour of Lead—
> Remembered, if outlived,
> As Freezing persons, recollect the Snow—
> First–Chill–then Stupor–then the letting go—[1]

Sportswriter Brian Phillips describes this state, which he experienced once when stranded for several hours on an icepack in the Bering Strait. "It was the first time I ever understood why freezing to death is sometimes described as . . . *just like falling asleep* . . . . It was like certain parts of [my] body just accrued this strange hush."² I recognize the temptation to lay down the burden of living, because I felt it when my body metabolized crushed OxyContin. I left my body and went elsewhere as my bodymind knew the strange rushing hush of nonbeing. Nodding off, I experienced the relief from my suffering as complete . . . myself gathered into a blissful absence of pain, below zero on the pain scale. Lovely, easeful, unsustainable, unlivable life.

Janet's told me how deeply relieved she was when I greeted her with "Hi, Jake" the second day she came to visit me in the ICU, where I had emerged from deep sedation. She further reports that the second thing I said was, "How was your conference?" In so doing, I immediately recognized her and her projects. She was reassured. I had a spinal cord injury, she had no idea what that would bring, but I knew her for herself and wanted to hear about her work. In other words, I was myself, which, in turn, helped her to recover a sense of who she was that had been terribly shaken over the preceding forty-eight hours. Our lives are intertwined, and my life is not mine alone, but shared with her. My living makes her life better, and she tells me so—it's that simple and that profound. I think it's accurate to call my injuries "catastrophic," and it's a testament to the sheer durability of our feelings for each other that the love that was so vital and alive before the accident survived without a scratch. This fact, more than any other, makes my inexpressibly difficult life livable, and I know that Janet and I enjoy a reciprocity of feeling that's very precious to us both.

Writing, no matter about what subject, has its way with the writer. Writing helps to teach us what we can't know otherwise, which makes it a demanding and invaluable discipline. Writing offers, not a way out, but a way into the impossible dilemmas of not-knowing. Each sentence begun can wander off, sometimes irretrievably into confusion and mistake, sometimes to greater clarity. Tropes transport memories and transform them, as resin is transformed under pressure into amber, sometimes with a small, ancient bit of life suspended inside. Amber can be remarkably clear, but the piece that conserves a suspended life is often more valuable. Writing works on memory, compressing and doubtless distorting the past, and offers bodies for the inspection of reader and writer alike.

Writing has turned me in ways I didn't know I was going to go—outward as well as inward. Attending to my family led toward a particular intimacy with my brother, Jeff, with whom I shared so much. Searching to represent unfathomable experience—both his and mine—has sent me repeatedly to the dictionary and to the concentrated language of lyric poetry, to ways of knowing like phenomenology and psychoanalysis that seek to understand human subjectivity, and to feminist and queer thinking about embodied and relational life. I've reached backward in memory to my childhood and young adulthood, but the process of writing has taken me forward, and continues to do so. Sentences unfold before me, always into the future, even as I return and work over what's already there.

I understand that every day I'm faced with an impossible choice—remembrance of things past or living on into a future that is troubling, even terrifying, but nonetheless underdetermined. I don't know what is going to happen, and I can't forget the past. I won't. I need it, I want and I need to remember the body that I once was. That body has suffered grievous injury, and to believe in myself as a strong, competent, and desirable woman I built on my memories of the many moments when I felt all that. Forgetting is impossible.

Forgetting is also imperiously necessary. In order to live on I must actively forget the person I once was, and be committed to forgetting more mindfully than you probably are as you go about your daily life. I am no longer what I once was—yet come to think of it, neither are you. All of us who live on are not what we were, but are becoming, always becoming. I have chosen, and for the immediately foreseeable future, will choose, to live as fully and passionately as I can. Every time I make that choice, I move further from the past, and am increasingly detached from what once was. It's a taxing process.

When I was rehabilitating at the Hospital for Special Care, paralysis had so weakened my hands that I couldn't turn a page of the Penguin paperbacks that line the bookshelves in my study. As you know, I was unable even to grasp a Kleenex and move it from right to left on my tray table, when Patty instructed me to do so. I cried tears of despair and rage, bitter tears. Day after day in therapy, I very slowly strengthened my grip as I followed her instructions. Several months after she had tried the tissue, Patty returned with a pencil and a book. She opened the book flat before me, and holding the pencil with the eraser facing outward, used it to grab the edge of a page. She turned it over. Then she handed the pencil to me. I grasped it with all my strength, and as Janet and my nurse, Winnie, watched, I turned a page. "I have my life back," I said with tears overflowing. I said again, "I have my life back," and we all four cried together.

ACKNOWLEDGMENTS

Paralysis and pain have impressed on me something that I knew before breaking my neck, but understand now with vivid clarity—the simple and profound fact of human interdependence. I have been since my accident so long dependent on so many that a listing of proper names cannot possibly represent all those who aided in my recovery and ongoing life. Nor can I single out all who rendered me extraordinary aid, again because the list would grow beyond measure, but I remember, and I am forever grateful. I remain indebted to every person who helped me and Janet in the sustained crisis and to the many who continue to ease my way. This debt is not one that I can discharge, because it is beyond calculation, nor is it a burden from which I wish to be relieved. I owe my life to a veritable host of people.

At the Hospital for Special Care:

Doctor Subramani Seetharama, my physiatrist, who said to Janet, "We are looking for positives here";

Danielle O'Connell, my life-affirming physical therapist;

Patty D'Arena, my empathetic and athletically accomplished occupational therapist;

Winnie Benjamin, my skilled and compassionate nurse;

Robyn Cop, a force of nature and integral part of the spinal cord injury team;

Jeff Dion, then head of the Connecticut Chapter of the National Spinal Cord Association, who came twice to the hospital when asked by Danielle, and convincingly demonstrated to me that it was possible to build a livable life after a cervical spinal cord injury; and

Donna Collier, who as a CNA carefully tended me in the hospital. She has continued lovingly to aid me, Monday through Friday, at home, and says every day in parting, "Call me if you need me." I do.

And at home on the weekends:

Shannon Upshur, handsome and charismatic, who lifts my spirits and pleases Moxie no end.

Early readers of the manuscript, each of whom helped me see more clearly what the book was and what it might be, and thereby encouraged me to keep writing:

Judy Butler
Joshua Takano Chambers-Letson
Lisa Cohen
Leigh Gilmore
Laura Grappo
Laura Levitt
Maggie Nelson
Tavia Nyong'o
Ann Pellegrini
Gayle Pemberton
Jord/ana Rosenberg
Gayle Salamon (thanks to Joan Scott for the introduction)
Matt Sharpe
Elizabeth Weed
Eric Zinner

Cecelia Cancellaro of Idea Architects, acting as my agent, persuasively represented the book to publishers and put me in the best possible position as an author with choices to make.

Friends and colleagues who helped both Janet and me in a myriad of ways large and small as we slowly built a livable life—many are also part of the Wesleyan community that continues to support my working life:

Henry Abelove
Rachel Adams
Susan Adler
Karen Anderson
Sally Bachner
Douglas Bennet
Midge Bennet
Elizabeth Bernstein
Laura Berry
Elizabeth Bobrick
Elizabeth Budnitz
Carole Bufithis
Elizabeth Castelli
Carolyn Coates
Robert Conn
Hope Dector
Ann DuCille
Lisa Duggan
David Eng
Allen Funk
E. Grace Glenny
Ray Gorneault
Lori Gruen
Kim F. Hall

David Hopson
Sybil Houlding
Gertrude Hughes
Allan Punzalan Isaac
Craig Jakobsen
Emily Jakobsen
Jane and James Jakobsen
Tom Jakobsen
Rebecca Jordan-Young
Kerwin Kaye
Natasha Korda
Juliana Kubala
Gale Lackey
Linda March
Elizabeth McAlister
Sean McCann
Lily Milroy
Margaret Neale
Ellen Nerenberg
Laurie Nussdorfer
Richard Ohmann
Migdalia Pinkney
Teresa Rankin
Mary-Jane Rubenstein
Teemu Ruskola
Anu (Aradhana) Sharma
Ann-Lou Shapiro
Bill Stowe
Andy Szegedy-Masak
Neferti Tadiar
Karin Trainer

Anthony Valerio
David Harrington Watt
Ruth Striegel Weissman

In addition to those listed above, I am particularly indebted to all the faculty and staff members of the English Department and the Feminist, Gender, and Sexuality Studies Program at Wesleyan and to the staff of the Barnard Center for Research on Women. My students have for many decades declared that another and better world is possible, and have immeasurably lifted my spirits.

The members of my extended family, who love and support me:

Beth Crosby
Colin Crosby
Kirsten Crosby Blose
Matt Blose
Andrea Molina
Kathy Kauffman
Barbara Martin
J. D. Martin
Nancy Cassel Stein

Notes

CHAPTER 1. YOUR PUNY, VULNERABLE SELF

1 See Judith Butler, *Precarious Life* (New York: Verso, 2004).
2 Maggie Nelson, "Morning En Route to the Hospital," in *Something Bright, Then Holes* (New York: Soft Skull Press, 2007), 42.
3 Emily Dickinson, "After great pain, a formal feeling comes–" (ca. 1862), *Poetry Foundation*, http://www.poetryfoundation.org/poem/177118, accessed July 3, 2015.

CHAPTER 3. BEWILDERMENT

1 See Judith Butler, *Giving an Account of Oneself* (New York: Fordham University Press, 2005).

CHAPTER 4. FALLING INTO HELL

1 Elaine Scarry, *The Body in Pain: The Making and Unmaking of the World* (Oxford: Oxford University Press, 1985), 4, 5.
2 Elizabeth Grosz, *The Volatile Body* (Bloomington: Indiana University Press, 1995).

CHAPTER 5. CARING AT THE CASH NEXUS

1 Lauren Berlant, *Cruel Optimism* (Durham, NC: Duke University Press, 2011).
2 Eduardo Porter, "Unionizing the Bottom of the Pay Scale," *New York Times*, December 5, 2012, http://www.nytimes.com/2012/12/05/business/unionizing-at-the-low-end-of-the-pay-scale.html, accessed March 7, 2015.
3 See Richard Kline, *Cigarettes Are Sublime* (Durham, NC: Duke University Press, 1995).
4 Langston Hughes, *The Ways of White Folk* (1934; New York: Vintage Classics, 1990).
5 Premilla Nadasen and Tiffany Williams, *Valuing Domestic Work*, New Feminist Solutions, vol. 5 (New York: Barnard Center for Research on Women, 2009), http://bcrw.barnard.edu/wp-content/nfs/reports/NFS5-Valuing-Domestic-Work.pdf, accessed March 6, 2015.

CHAPTER 6. LOST IN SPACE

1 See Sara Ahmed, *Queer Phenomenology: Orientation, Objects, Others* (Durham, NC: Duke University Press, 2006).

2 See Gayle Salamon, *Assuming a Body: Transgender and Rhetorics of Materiality* (New York: Columbia University Press, 2010).

CHAPTER 7. MASCULINE, FEMININE, OR FOURTH OF JULY

1 Ann Fausto-Sterling, *Sexing the Body: Gender Politics and the Construction of Sexuality* (New York: Basic Books, 2000).

2 S. Bear Bergman, *The Nearest Exit May Be Behind You* (Vancouver: Arsenal Pulp Press, 2009), 20.

3 See Gayle Salamon, *The Life and Death of Latisha King: A Phenomenology* (New York: NYU Press, forthcoming).

4 Leslie Feinberg, *Stone Butch Blues: A Novel* (1993; New York: Alyson Books, 2003); Elizabeth Lapovsky Kennedy and Madeline D. Davis, *Boots of Leather, Slippers of Gold: The History of a Lesbian Community*, twentieth anniversary edition (1993; New York: Routledge, 2014).

5 "Katmandou," *Lost Womyn's Space*, http://lostwomynsspace.blogspot. com/2011/07/katmandou.html, accessed May 31, 2015.

6 "Rocky Horror Picture Show Lyrics," *Metrolyrics*, http://www.metrolyrics. com/the-time-warp-lyrics-rocky-horror-picture-show.html, accessed October 7, 2014.

CHAPTER 8. TIME HELD ME GREEN AND DYING

1 "Drafting," *Exploratorium's Science of Cycling*, http://www.exploratorium.edu/ cycling/aerodynamics2.html, accessed March 1, 2013.

2 Dylan Thomas, "Fern Hill" (1945), in *The Poems of Dylan Thomas* (New York: New Directions, 1952); available at *Poets.org*, http://www.poets.org/poetsorg/ poem/fern-hill, accessed July 20, 2015.

CHAPTER 10. VIOLENCE AND THE SACRED

1 René Girard, *Violence and the Sacred* (1972; Baltimore: Johns Hopkins University Press, 1977), 28.

2 Sigmund Freud, "The 'Uncanny'" (1919), *MIT.edu*, http://web.mit.edu/ allanmc/www/freud1.pdf, 3, 1–2, accessed June 28, 2015.

3 Philip Larkin, "This Be the Verse" (1971), in *Collected Poems* (New York: Farrar, Straus and Giroux, 2001); available at *Poetry Foundation*, http://www. poetryfoundation.org/poem/178055, accessed September 15, 2012.

CHAPTER 11. BOWELS LEAD

1 "Defecation," *Encyclopedia Britannica*, http://www.britannica.com/
EBchecked/topic/155613/defecation, accessed November 29, 2014.

2 W. H. Auden, "The Geography of the House" (1964), in *Collected
Poems* (1976; London: Faber and Faber, 1994); available at *Poem Hunter*,
http://www.poemhunter.com/poem/the-geography-of-the-house/, accessed
July 20, 2015.

CHAPTER 12. I'M YOUR PHYSICAL LOVER

1 Maggie Nelson, "Halo Over the Hospital," in *Something Bright, Then Holes*
(New York: Soft Skull Press, 2007), 46–47, 44–45.

2 Maurice Merleau-Ponty, *Phenomenology of Perception* (London: Routledge,
2002), 197.

3 "Ambiguous," *Oxford English Dictionary*, vol. I, ed. J. A. Simpson and E.S.C.
Weiner (Oxford: Clarendon Press, 1989), 386.

4 Merleau-Ponty, *Phenomenology of Perception*, 198.

5 Judith Halberstam, *Female Masculinity* (Durham, NC: Duke University Press,
1993).

6 Angela Carter, *The Bloody Chamber* (1979; New York: Penguin, 1993), 19.

CHAPTER 13. SUPPLY AND DEMAND

1 William Blake, "A Poison Tree" (1794), *Poetry Foundation*, http://www.
poetryfoundation.org/poem/175222, accessed February 2, 2013.

CHAPTER 14. SHAMELESS HUSSY, BABE D., MOXIE DOXIE

1 "Doxy," *Oxford English Dictionary*, vol. IV, ed. J. A. Simpson and E.S.C.
Weiner (Oxford: Clarendon Press, 1989), 1004.

2 "Hussy," *Compact Edition of the Oxford English Dictionary*, vol. I, ed. J.A.H.
Murray et al. (Oxford: Oxford University Press, 1971), 1353.

CHAPTER 15. ANABAPTIST REFORMATIONS

1 William Wordsworth, "The World Is Too Much with Us; Late and Soon"
(1806), in *The Complete Poetical Works* (London: Macmillan and Co., 1888);
available at *Bartleby.com*, http://www.bartleby.com/145/ww317.html, accessed
February 28, 2012.

2 David Harrington Watt, *Bible-Carrying Christians: Conservative Protestants
and Social Power* (New York: Oxford University Press, 2002).

3 "Caritas," *Oxford English Dictionary*, vol. II, ed. J. A. Simpson and E.S.C. Weiner (Oxford: Clarendon Press, 1989), 900.

4 Charlotte Brontë, *Jane Eyre*, third edition (1848; New York: W. W. Norton & Company, 2001), 253. Brontë is quoting Psalm 69, 1–2, in the voice of Jane, her first-person heroine-narrator.

CHAPTER 16. PRETTY, WITTY, AND GAY

1 "Addict," *American Heritage Dictionary*, ed. William Morris (New York: Houghton Mifflin, 1978), 15.

2 Elaine Freedgood, *The Ideas in Things: Fugitive Meaning in the Victorian Novel* (Chicago: University of Chicago Press, 2006), 32.

CHAPTER 17. THE HORROR! THE HORROR!

1 Elizabeth Ermarth, *Realism and Consensus in the English Novel* (Princeton, NJ: Princeton University Press, 1998).

2 Peter Brooks, *Reading for the Plot: Design and Intention in Narrative* (New York: Alfred A. Knopf, 1985), 23, 323.

3 Susan Stewart, "The Epistemology of the Horror Story," *Journal of American Folklore* 95.375 (January–March 1982): 35–36.

4 Edgar Allan Poe, "The Fall of the House of Usher" (1839), *Literature Network*, http://www.online-literature.com/poe/31/, accessed June 26, 2011.

5 Otto Kernberg, "Some Observations on the Process of Mourning," *International Journal of Psychoanalysis* 91.3 (June 2010): 601–619.

CHAPTER 18. LIVING ON

1 Emily Dickinson, "After great pain, a formal feeling comes–" (ca. 1862), *Poetry Foundation*, http://www.poetryfoundation.org/poem/177118, accessed July 3, 2015.

2 Brian Phillips, "Out in the Great Alone," *Grantland (ESPN.com)*, May 5, 2013, http://espn.go.com/espn/feature/story/_/id/9175394/out-great-alone, accessed June 8, 2015.

About the Author

Christina Crosby, Professor of English and Feminist, Gender, and Sexuality Studies at Wesleyan University, is the author of *The Ends of History: Victorians and "The Woman Question"* and essays on other Victorian and feminist topics. She is broadly interested in queer and feminist work in disability studies and studies of embodiment. Her current project is exploring "my body electric" as both a rhetorically perverse catachresis and a literal neurological fact.

SEXUAL CULTURES

General Editors: Ann Pellegrini, Tavia Nyong'o, and Joshua Chambers-Letson

Founding Editors: José Esteban Muñoz and Ann Pellegrini

Titles in the series include the following:

For a complete list of books in the series, see www.nyupress.org.